WHY STAY
CATHOLIC?

Other Books by Michael Leach

I Like Being Catholic
I Like Being Married
I Like Being American
A Maryknoll Book of Prayer
A Maryknoll Book of Inspiration

WHY STAY
CATHOLIC?

Unexpected Answers to a Life-Changing Question

MICHAEL LEACH

LOYOLA PRESS.
A JESUIT MINISTRY
Chicago

LOYOLA PRESS.
A JESUIT MINISTRY

3441 N. Ashland Avenue
Chicago, Illinois 60657
(800) 621-1008
www.loyolapress.com

Photo credits: MT Winter photo p. 152 courtesy of Medical Mission Sisters. Thea Bowman photo p. 166 courtesy of Franciscan Sisters of Perpetual Adoration. Pat Reardon photo p. 172 by Mark Solock. Bob McCahill photo p. 178 © Sean Sprague. John Smyth photo p. 198 by Bill Watson. Dorothy Day photo p. 214 courtesy of Marquette University Archives. Bishop Raymond Lucker photo p. 222 courtesy of The Catholic Spirit. Old St. Patrick's Church photo p. 268 courtesy of Old St. Patrick's. P. 274 [Gethsemani] photo © Gavin Richardson. P. 282 [Catholic Charities] photo © Duncan Sprott. P. 288 [Catholic schools] photo courtesy Convent of the Sacred Heart, Greenwich, CT. P. 296 [Catholic hospitals] photo courtesy of St. Joseph Hospital, Orange, CA. P. 304 [Catholic Extension Society] photo courtesy Catholic Extension Society. P. 312 [Catholic Relief Services] photo © Sean Sprague. P. 322 [Catholic bookstore] photo © Laura Kolb. P. 330 [LA Congress] photo courtesy Los Angeles Religious Education Congress. P. 336 [street signs] photo © Fotosearch. P. 343 [Sidewalk forgiveness] photo by Steve Connor.

Cover design by Jill Arena
Interior design by Donna Antkowiak

Library of Congress Cataloging-in-Publication Data
Leach, Michael, 1940-
  Why stay Catholic? : unexpected answers to a life-changing question / Michael Leach.
    p. cm.
  ISBN-13: 978-0-8294-3537-5
  ISBN-10: 0-8294-3537-9
  1. Catholic Church--Apologetic works. 2. Catholic Church--Membership. I. Title.
  BX1752.L42 2011
  230'.2--dc22

                                                                2010048634

Printed in the United States of America
11 12 13 14 15 16 17 18 Bang 10 9 8 7 6 5 4 3 2

For Father Greeley,
of course.

Contents

PART 2: People

PART 3: Places

Preface

Frustrated with the Catholic Church? Don't despair! Be of good cheer! There is another way of looking at things. This book is for you:

+ Cradle Catholics who love the church but are embarrassed by too many scandals and too many cover-ups;
+ Recovering Catholics who have been hurt by the church but wouldn't mind a reminder of the beautiful things they miss;
+ Weary Catholics who are tired of hearing the same sermons week after week, who wonder where the beef is and whether they should just stay in bed;
+ Ex-Catholics—the fastest growing religion in America—who are interested in spirituality but still haven't found it;
+ Non-Catholics who wonder what's so great about this flawed church that most Catholics wouldn't even leave it if they were kicked out.

Why Stay Catholic? responds to the questions: Why stay in the church? and What's so good about being Catholic anyway? Its message is, "Don't throw the baby out with the bathwater!" The baby is precious, it's real, it never grows old, can still give you joy, peace, and assurance, and it's not dependent on people.

One story has it that Napoleon once told a cardinal that he could destroy the Catholic Church with his fists, in an instant, if he wanted to. The Cardinal laughed and said, "We clergy have been trying to destroy the church for eighteen hundred years with our sins and stupidity but haven't come close. What makes you think you can do better?"

We live in a dualistic world. "The world is charged with the grandeur of God," the poet Hopkins reminds us, but it's also riddled with opposites: good and bad; hot and cold; pleasure and pain; happy and sad; war and peace; rich and poor; black and white; Democrat and Republican; Abbot and Costello; Red Sox and Yankee; the joy of victory and the agony of defeat; you name it, or not. Fortunately, we have Christ's promise: "In this world you shall have trial and tribulation, but be of good cheer, for I have overcome the world!" (John 16:33)

This is a book about some of the good stuff in Catholicism. The beef. What Teilhard de Chardin called "the chosen part of things," what Hopkins saw as "the dearest freshness deep down things." It's about the things that last because they are spiritual.

So put aside the portrait of the church you see on television—it's incomplete, like a *Mona Lisa* without a smile, or a *Pieta* without an embrace. The purpose of this book is to bring the smile back to Catholicism, the kind that comes from deep in your heart, and to remind you of the embrace, the one you don't always see but is closer to you than breathing and nearer than hands and feet.

Michael Leach

PART 1

Ideas

The Catholic Church speaks of the "deposit of faith," a phrase that points to beliefs and practices deposited by men and women in Catholic consciousness for the past two thousand years. Strictly speaking, it refers to a number of Scriptures and traditions as interpreted by bishops and popes, but spiritually seen, it's an open vault so large and deep that no one can withdraw all of its riches in a thousand lifetimes. The deposit of faith is not a limited checking account; it's a trust fund that increases and multiplies.

What is the gold standard in the deposit of faith? Ideas that point to spiritual realities. Many of them have been forgotten or ignored for too long. Here are just a few. Smile and know the embrace.

1

The Sacramental Imagination

Though I was blind, now I see.
—JOHN 9:25

Being a Catholic is about seeing the chosen part of things.

✛ An infant whose Father's house has many mansions but who chooses to be born in a manger.
✛ A man nailed to a cross who is not a victim but unbounded love.
✛ A virgin womb. A faithful groom. An empty tomb.
✛ A treasure hidden in a field. A coin found. A mustard seed.
✛ Eternity in a grain of sand.

Catholicism is about seeing what the eyes cannot see and understanding what is at the heart of things: truth, love, mercy, goodness, beauty, harmony, humility, compassion, gratitude, joy, peace, salvation. It's about seeing the ordinary and perceiving the extraordinary at the same time: the midnight glow of Easter candles that are, in truth, a thousand points of light; the stories of saints, the saga of sinners, and the rumors of angels that inspire and heal us. "It is only with the heart that one sees rightly," wrote Antoine de Saint-Exupery. "What is essential is invisible to the eye."

We don't choose to see the chosen parts of things. It chooses us. It's like when we gaze at the silhouette of a vase. Sometimes we see the vase; then instantly we see two faces. Which is real; which is true? We can't force ourselves to see either one. Both are there. What we see in the moment chooses us.

We see water running down an infant's head at baptism, and suddenly we behold new life. We watch a priest or a sister or a layperson handing out wafers but are aware that God's spiritual child is sharing God's spiritual life with God's spiritual children—and we know that all are somehow mysteriously one. We look at a holy card, a piece of paper, and perceive fidelity, courage, and love. What first appears ordinary catches fire. The mundane turns to gold. A divine alchemy takes place. We see the chosen parts: beauty, love, harmony, joy. This is what is called the "sacramental imagination."

A sacrament points to and opens what is invisible but real. It is an outward sign, instituted by Christ, to give grace. Catholics cherish the seven sacraments of the Church: baptism, confirmation, Holy Communion, reconciliation, marriage, holy orders, and the anointing of the sick. These are the Sacraments with a big *S*. There are also sacraments with a small *s*. We receive the Sacraments once or many times over a lifetime. But we give sacraments every moment of our lives.

✞ We give a sacrament of baptism every time we behold another as a child of God.

✞ We offer a sacrament of reconciliation every time we say to someone "I'm sorry" or "I forgive you."

✞ Every time a wife says to her husband or a husband to his wife, "I love you"—or better, when a husband gets a cold cloth and puts it on his wife's forehead when she has a headache, or when a wife gives her husband a hug for no other reason than she knows he needs it—is a sacrament of marriage.

✞ A sacrament of eucharist happens every time family or friends gather around a table to share in the good of God.

✞ Every time someone decides to live a better life is a sacrament of confirmation.

✞ Everyone who makes a radical commitment to be here not for himself but for God expresses a sacrament of holy orders.

✞ Every time we visit a sick person in a hospital or nursing home and just kiss them on the cheek is an anointing of the sick.

What could be more beautiful?

An old song says, "Little things mean a lot." Sacraments with a small *s* mean everything to those who give them and to those who receive them.

Catholicism is about cultivating our sacramental imagination so that we can see and be the chosen part of things.

"Catholicism is above all a way of seeing," writes theologian Robert Barron in his book *And Now I See.* "Origen of Alexandria once remarked that holiness is seeing with the eyes of Christ. Teilhard de Chardin said, with great passion, that his mission as a Christian thinker was to help people see, and Thomas Aquinas said that the ultimate goal of the Christian life is a 'beatific vision', an act of seeing."

When I was in seminary studying to be a priest, our English teacher, Fr. Ignatius Burrill, introduced us to the poetry of Gerard Manley Hopkins. He opened my eyes to a sacramental world of beauty beyond words. I'll always remember this verse:

Christ plays in ten thousand places,
Lovely in limbs, and lovely in eyes not his
To the Father through the features of men's faces.

When I was at home that summer, I saw Christ on Clark Street. I was walking toward our apartment near Wrigley Field and passed a down-and-out guy drinking from a bottle in a paper bag. I didn't look him in the eyes. Then I recalled my friend Larry McCauley telling me about a church not far from both of us with a crucified Jesus etched in stone on the wall. A legend under the cross read, "Is it nothing to you who pass by?" Suddenly the man on the street and the man on the cross were one.

Later I saw a little girl playing jacks on the sidewalk in front of her house. She playfully tossed the jacks on the pavement just as God must have flung the stars across the sky. She bounced the little red ball, and it paused in the air as if it were the sun. I thought I was seeing the whole story of creation in a game of jacks.

I looked at many people on my way home that day but saw them differently than I ever had before. Each of them wore a human face, etched in stone or as sunny as July, and each revealed a unique face of Christ. Hopkins's words appeared and disappeared. I saw a person, and I saw who was really there.

As soon as the moment came, just as soon did it go. But I remember it still.

There comes a moment, once—and God help those
Who pass that moment by!—when Beauty stands
looking into the soul with grave, sweet eyes
That sicken at pretty words.

—CYRANO DE BERGERAC

Fr. Burrill and Larry McCauley taught me that poetry is the best theology. The sacramental imagination, a unique Catholic idea, opens our inner eye to the chosen part of things. St. Bonaventure, a father of the church, counseled his students to "see with the eyes of the soul." The mystic Meister Eckhart said that "we see God with the same eyes that God sees us." Everything is somehow one. "If you have an eye for it," St. Augustine wrote, "the world itself is a sacrament."

"The sacramental imagination" is a phrase popularized by Fr. Andrew Greeley. He adapted it from the theology of his friend Fr. David Tracy, a theologian at the

Divinity School of the University of Chicago, who wrote a seminal book called *The Analogical Imagination*. Fr. Greeley writes in his book, *The Catholic Imagination*:

> Catholics live in an enchanted world, a world of statues and holy water, stained glass and votive candles, saints and religious medals, rosary beads and holy pictures. But these Catholic paraphernalia are mere hints of a deeper and more pervasive religious sensibility which inclines Catholics to see the Holy lurking in creation. As Catholics, we find our houses and our world haunted by a sense that the objects, events and persons of daily life are revelations of grace. (p. 1)

Catholicism, seen through the eye of a needle, is a religion of rules and regulations. Seen with the sacramental imagination, it is a unique take on life, a holy vision, a way of seeing the chosen part of things.

When asked who he was and what he did, Jesus told his disciples, "Come and *see!*" Who can resist an invitation like that?

2

God Is Everywhere

Q. Where is God?
A. Everywhere!
—THE BALTIMORE CATECHISM

A tattered copy of this standard text sat on the desk of every girl and boy in Catholic schools from 1885 till the late 1960s. You will not find a Catholic adult who cannot repeat that remarkable Q and A. It's a simple expression of faith that points to the chosen part of *everything*.

I was surprised not to find anything like it in the new *Catechism of the Catholic Church*, but that may just be me. *The Baltimore Catechism* was a sixty-two-page booklet, and the Vatican catechism has 928 pages and weighs more than my brain. I did find the word *omnipotence* five times in the index but no mention of the word *omnipresence*. I thought, *Gee, this is like having a classic songbook of the Beatles that doesn't include "Here, There, and Everywhere."* On the other hand, *The Baltimore Catechism* doesn't tell us what Easter is about. It's helpful to have more than one catechism in the house.

9

That's because we can never hear enough of this wonderful Catholic idea: God is everywhere. We know from the movie, *The Big Lebowski*, that the Dude abides but we know from Scripture and tradition that Grace abounds. Grace runs through everything because God is "here, there, and everywhere." What could be more comforting?

> *Wither shall I go from thy spirit? Or wither shall I flee from thy presence? If I ascend up into heaven, thou art there: if I make my bed in hell, behold thou art there. If I take the wings of the morning, and dwell in the uttermost parts of the sea, even there shall thy hand lead me and thy right hand shall hold me.*
> —PSALM 139:7–10, KJV

> *Yea, though I walk through the valley of the shadow of death, I will fear no evil: for thou art with me; thy rod and thy staff they comfort me.*
> —PSALM 23:4, KJV

At the end of the novel *Diary of a Country Priest* a young priest lies dying, waiting for an old pastor to arrive and administer last rites. The friend at his bedside worries that the pastor won't get there on time and the priest will not receive the church's last blessing. The dying priest senses his concern and, in a halting but clear voice, says, "Does it matter? Grace is everywhere."

The church may not always be there for us, but Catholicism teaches that God is everywhere for us. That's all that matters.

Jesus taught us to look for God in the birds of the air and the lilies of the field. When I was a young priest (I left after three years to marry), I once said a Mass for children who were sitting in a field of dandelions next to a lake with frogs popping out like Muppets. I read the gospel on the lilies of the field and then asked the children: "Each one of you, go and choose a flower and just look at it." They scattered and each found a pet dandelion and put their face close to it. "Just look at it," I said. "And see how it grows." The children smiled as the yellow lions smiled back. I waited. I whispered, "If I could look into your eyes right now, I would see a flower. God is everywhere, and each of you is baptizing a flower!"

> The fullness of joy is to behold God in everything.
> —St. Julian of Norwich

Shortest sermon I ever gave.

Finding God in all things is the foundation of Ignatian spirituality. But to say that God is in all things is not to say that everything is God. That would be pantheism, literally "All *is* God." God and creation are not the same. God is greater than the sum of all the parts of all that he has made. "God is All in all" (1 Corinthians 15:28), "God is love" (1 John 4:8), and, incredibly, "We live and move and have our being in God" (Acts 17:28).

> The day of my spiritual wakening was the day I saw—and knew I saw—all things in God and God in all things.
> —Mechtild of Magdeburg

These words spark our sacramental imagination and help us understand an awesome truth. We are like fish that swim in an ocean of love: the fish are in the ocean, and the ocean is in the fish. We are in God and God is in us. We are swimming in God but don't even know it. The key to peace—and to swimming effortlessly through life—is to come to know who and where we really are. God is love, God is everywhere, and everywhere is in God. Wherever we are, God is always present! We don't have to look far to find God. He is within us and all around us because we are within him. This idea has tremendous practical applications for prayer and daily living.

Here is what religious educator Michael Morwood has to say about the God who is so everywhere that "the heavens and the heavens above the heavens cannot contain him" (Psalm 68:33):

> It makes a big difference how we pray if we view God as a person in heaven or, as the *Baltimore Catechism* put it, if we view God "everywhere." For many of us prayer has been an effort to contact an "elsewhere God." What happens when we shift our attention to an "everywhere God"—a sustaining Presence in all, through all, never absent, never distant, not in one place more than in any other place, a Presence "in whom we live and move and have our being"?
>
> There is a new story emerging in consciousness, one that evokes awe, wonder, and reverence as it expands our notion of God. We are beginning to understand that God is not limited to a place and only vaguely present in the universe. We are beginning to appreciate a God alive in every particle in the billions of galaxies beyond us and in the grass or pavement beneath our feet. God is here, everywhere, and always with us.

May we open our minds and hearts
to the presence of God in us.
May God-in-us,
the "everywhere God,"
find generous and courageous expression
in our words and actions
as we undertake
to make the reign of God
evident in our world.
Amen.
(Michael Morwood, from *Praying a New Story*,
pp. 7, 138)

God is present in the furthest star and in the smallest seed. God is present before and after we are born and in every detail of our lives. God is love and wisdom and available to us in each and every moment because we are, literally, in love. It only takes eyes to see.

Did you ever see that wonderful black-and-white movie from the 1950s, *The Incredible Shrinking Man*? The hero, Scott Carey, blond, blue-eyed, and tall, is sailing his boat in the ocean beneath an infinite sky. Suddenly a mist appears and covers him with a radioactive dust. Slowly he goes from six feet to three feet to three inches to infinitesimal. At the end of the movie this dot of a man is walking in his garden through blades of grass that are taller than trees, amongst towering flowers that look like planets and suns, and sailing on a twig over a puddle as large as a lake. Suddenly, Scott *sees*. He is still at home in the universe! It has shrunk but God is everywhere. We hear his inner voice:

> So close—the infinitesimal and the infinite. But suddenly, I knew they were really the two ends of the same concept. The unbelievably small and the unbelievably vast eventually meet—like the closing of a gigantic circle. I looked up, as if somehow I would grasp the heavens. The universe, worlds beyond number, God's silver tapestry spread across the night. And in that moment, I knew the answer to the riddle of the infinite. I had thought in terms of man's own limited dimension. I had presumed upon nature. That existence begins and ends in man's conception, not nature's. And I felt my body dwindling, melting, becoming nothing. My fears melted away. And in their place came acceptance. All this vast majesty of creation, it had to mean something. And then I meant something, too! Yes, smaller than the smallest, I meant something, too. To God, there is no zero. I still exist!

The Catholic idea that God is everywhere is a source of infinite joy. God is love, and that's where we live. Love does not look down and judge. Love teaches us how to live among flowers and to swim in an ocean of love.

3

God Finds Us When
We Least Expect Him

*Christmas, Good Friday, Easter—their message is
not that we must appease an angry God but that
a God of love has found us!*
—THOMAS O'MEARA, OP, ATTRIBUTED

Isn't that wonderful! We don't have to look for God. God
is not only everywhere, but God is always finding us!

God finds us when we least expect him. He finds us
when we are lost in sin, and he finds us, too, when we're
lost in the sacrament of the present moment. This is a
beautiful idea expressed in Catholic poems and stories
throughout the ages. The deposit of faith is filled to overflowing with tales of God's love.

The poet Francis Thompson (1859–1907) writes beautifully about our flight from God and God's pursuit of us
in *The Hound of Heaven*:

I fled Him, down the nights and down the days;
I fled Him, down the arches of the years;
I fled Him, down the labyrinthine ways
   Of my own mind; and in the mist of tears
I hid from Him, and under running laughter.
        Up vistaed hopes I sped;
        And shot, precipitated,
Adown Titanic glooms of chasmèd fears,
From those strong Feet that followed, followed after.
        But with unhurrying chase,
        And unperturbèd pace,
    Deliberate speed, majestic instancy,
       They beat—and a Voice beat
       More instant than the Feet—
   "All things betray thee, who betrayest Me."

And finally, when we are out of breath and can run no more, we hear God's call:

   "Rise, clasp My hand, and come!"

. . .

   "Ah, fondest, blindest, weakest,
   I am He Whom thou seekest!
Thou dravest love from thee, who dravest Me!"

We can no more escape God than a wave can escape the ocean. The wave is in the ocean, and the ocean is in the wave. God is with us whether we want him to be or not. St. Augustine wrote, "Our hearts our restless until they rest in Thee." We will know salvation, sooner or later. Sooner is better.

The parable of the lost son (Luke 15:11–32) gives us assurance. A restless young man asks his affluent father for his share of the inheritance. The generous father gives it to him. The son goes off and squanders it, living a life of debauchery, sleeping with pigs and eating their swill. The prodigal son, like the lost soul in *The Hound of Heaven*, cries out, "I have recklessly forgotten Your glory, O Father!" He begins crawling back home, praying that his father will receive him as a penitent and let him back in the house, if only as a hired hand.

And here is the best part, the part that warms and enfolds us like a favorite quilt. Here is a reason that I am still Catholic:

> While he was still far off, his father saw him and was filled with compassion; he ran and put his arms around him and kissed him. Then the son said to him, "Father, I have sinned against heaven and before you; I am no longer worthy to be called your son." But the father said to his slaves, "Quickly, bring out a robe—the best one—and put it on him; put a ring on his finger and sandals on his feet. And get the fatted calf and kill it, and let us eat and celebrate; for this son of mine was dead and is alive again; he was lost and is found!" And they began to celebrate. (Luke 15:20–24, NRSV)

The father makes the first move! The father races to embrace the son before the son can say a word!

God finds us, again and again, when we least expect him. He finds us because he never left us, giving us everything always, and giving us even more when we recognize who we are and where Love is. Jesus assures us that God can never leave us: "I will not leave you orphaned. . . . I am in my Father, and you in me, and I in you." (John 14:18, 20). Repentance happens when we realize that we are in Jesus and that Jesus and the Father are *one* (John 10:30).

> If I ascend up into heaven, thou art there: if I make my bed in hell, behold, thou art there!
> —PSALM 139:8
>
> God's love for us is freely given and unearned, surpassing all we could ever hope for or imagine. He does not love us because we have merited it or are worthy of it. God loves us, rather, because he is true to his own nature.
> —POPE JOHN PAUL II

God is the Hound of heaven. He finds us in our despair. It makes no difference what we have done—God is already there. This is an idea from the deposit of faith that makes it easy for me to stay Catholic.

God not only finds us when we are lost; he also finds us when we aren't even looking for him. He finds us in the present moment. Long before Eckhart Tolle wrote *The Power of Now*, Jean-Pierre de Caussade, SJ (1675–1751) wrote *The Sacrament of the Present Moment*, and Brother Lawrence of the Resurrection's (c. 1611–1691) teachings were compiled in *Practice of the Presence of God*. In the first chapter of this book we learned about the

seven sacraments with a small *s*. The *eighth* sacrament—
the sacrament of the present moment—opens our eyes
to a God of surprises who comes to us when we least
expect him.

When Thomas Merton was a young monk at the Abbey
of Gethsemane, he sometimes had to go to Louisville for
a doctor's appointment. At first the hurrying crowds dis-
tracted him from his endeavor to pray always. But one day
Merton just let go. He stood still and looked. Suddenly the
whole city seemed to glow with the grace of God. "How do
you tell people," he asked himself, "that they are walking
around shining like the sun!"

That is a sacrament of the present moment.

In the movie *Field of Dreams* a tourist asks the hero,
Ray Kinsella, "Is this heaven?"

"No," he says. "It's Iowa."

Heaven begins on the spot where we are standing.
Funny thing, but like Ray, I think I first had a sense of
God's presence playing baseball. Let me tell you about it.

I was eight or nine years old. Maybe ten. It doesn't
matter, because when it happened, time stood still, and I
was eternal.

In my big-city neighborhood the kids played softball
on cross streets where manhole covers served as bases.
The fourteen-incher would pop its stitches, but you used
it until it was a pillow. Even so, you'd better not smack it
too far down the middle, or it might crack the window
of an apartment building. You had to pull the ball to the
street on the left or punch it down the street to the right.
You began playing after school and didn't stop until your

mother called your name from a wooden porch or the sun sank behind the skyline.

Little guys like me sat on the curb until one of the big guys put us in, usually on the street to the right. I'd often drop the ball, especially hard line drives, and rarely hit one past the pitcher. I wanted to play well and not goof up, and I thought about what the other kids were thinking of me. Then one evening (or more accurately this one sacramental moment) while the sun was painting the apartment windows gold, I stopped wanting, stopped thinking.

And heaven said hello.

I was in right field. The ball popped off the bat like grease from a frying pan and lofted high over my head. All I did was *see* it and turn and follow its path. I wasn't thinking about it. Just running, aware of each step, each move of my arms, as if in slow motion, knowing exactly where the ball would come down. At just the right moment, without looking, my fingers reached out and the softball fell onto my hands like a dove. I ran a few more steps, turned, held it up, and smiled!

The big guys cheered. Then the moment vanished.

But to this day, sixty years later, I can remember that golden instant when time stood still and I felt one with the ball, the sun, the street, and yes, let's say it, love.

God is love, an unbelievable oneness that comes to awareness when you least expect it: in the sacrament of the present moment. Baseball first taught me not to worry about the past or plan for the future but simply to pay attention to the ball. I'd need many reminders throughout my life, but I began to learn: God envelops us when we least expect it.

I don't remember what happened after that catch, but I remember other moments of oneness that came suddenly but never lasted more than an inning. Just as quickly as one came, I would take pride in it or dwell on it or try to do it again, and it was gone.

God finds us when we forget about ourselves and live in the present. Awareness catches *us*, but the moment falls apart when we try to pin it against the wall of our mind like a butterfly. It comes to us on colorful see-through wings. And as soon as we take credit for it, it vanishes.

But we never forget it.

Its promise keeps us going—and finds us again when we least expect it.

Everyone of every religion and of no religion has these wonderful moments. I grew up with them in a world of Catholic poems and stories and friends. Still Catholic? Why not?

4

Nothing Can Separate Us from the Love of God—*Nothing!*

Neither death, nor life, nor angels, nor rulers, nor things
present, nor things to come, nor powers, nor height, nor
depth, nor anything else in all creation, will be able to
separate us from the love of God in Christ Jesus our Lord!
—ROMANS 8:38–39, NRSV

What could be more beautiful? No matter what we do or how bad we think we are, nothing can separate us from the love of God. How could it? "We live and move and have our being in God" (Acts 17:28). Can anyone separate a wave from the ocean or a sunbeam from the sun? Catholicism teaches that we are literally in Jesus, and Jesus, who is one with the Father, is in us (John 14:18, 20). "We are syllables," wrote Caryll Houselander, "of the perfect Word!" "God hugs us," said Hildegarde of Bingen. "We are encircled by the arms of the mystery of God."

When Jesus saved the adulteress about to be stoned, he didn't say, "Sin no more and I will not condemn you." He said, "I do not condemn you. *Now* go and sin no more." We first experience God's embrace, and *then* our life changes forever. It all begins with a spiritual idea. Can there be a more joy-making idea than this one?

I saw a beautiful demonstration of this idea at a Catholic convention many years ago. Late at night I took the hotel elevator to a floor where the host organization had a hospitality suite for the conference speakers, a who's who of Catholicism. People packed the room in clusters, ice crackling in cocktail glasses, smoke swirling from cigarettes. My eyes immediately went to the far corner of the room where a nun sat on a sofa, a thin young man resting his head on her chest. The Sister was Jeannine Gramick, a friend whose book on ministering to gays and lesbians in the church I had just published. The boy was so thin, and he seemed so sad. I wondered: does he have AIDS? Jeannine touched his hair with her fingers, gently, like the feathers of an angel. I thought for a moment that someone had moved the *Pieta* from St. Peter's Basilica to this hotel on the outskirts of Chicago. I was aware that the institutional church did not go out of its way to embrace gay Catholics, and I could not take my eyes off this Catholic Sister who was demonstrating—quietly, without fanfare, in the corner of a room—the basic Catholic truth that nothing can separate us from the love of God—*nothing*.

Just as nothing can separate us from the love of God—not death, not sin, not anything—nothing can separate us from one another. We are literally one with one another. When Jesus said, "Love your neighbor as yourself," I think he meant it literally. We *are* our neighbor, and our neighbor is *us*. Jesus said, "I and my Father are one," and then went on to teach us how to pray by saying, "*Our* Father . . ." We are all, each of us, brothers and sisters, children of God, made in the image and likeness of love. What could be more beautiful?

Vickie and I used to go to the Saturday evening Mass at a small working-class par-ish miles from our home. The church had as many people kneeling in the pews as Wrigley Field has fans sitting in the bleachers during a thunderstorm. But the few people who did attend went there for one reason. The priest gave the same sermon, in different words, every single Saturday of the year. He preached the everlasting love of God in Jesus Christ. His words weren't fancy, but they were authentic. He meant what he said. The parishioners could not get enough.

Did you know that the passage that leads off this chap-ter appears many times in the Catholic lectionary? We cannot hear it enough.

This passage is the second reading on the eighteenth Sunday in Ordinary Time, Year A. You will also hear it on the weekday of the thirtieth week in Ordinary Time. It also appears in the Proper of Saints, numbers 538, 592, and 642a. Not to mention in Commons, number 716. Did I forget to mention that it also appears in Ritual Masses,

> The love of Christ is more powerful than sin and death. St. Paul explains that Christ came to forgive sin, and that his love is greater than any sin, stronger than all my personal sins or those of anyone else. This is the faith of the Church. This is the Good News of God's love that the Church proclaims throughout history, and that I proclaim to you today: God loves you with an everlasting love. He loves you in Christ Jesus, his Son.
> —POPE JOHN PAUL II

numbers 792 and 802, in Masses for Various Needs, numbers 863 and 869, and in Masses for the Dead, number 1014?

When is the last time you heard or, if you are a priest, gave a sermon on, "Nothing can separate us from the love of God?" It's one of the most neglected ideas in our spiritual deposit of faith.

And it's one of the best reasons I can think of for anyone to say, "I am still Catholic."

5

God's Will for Us Is More Wonderful Than Anything We Can Imagine

Q: Why did God make you?
A: He made me to know him, to love him, and to serve him
in this world, and to be happy with him forever in heaven.
—THE BALTIMORE CATECHISM

God, infinitely perfect and blessed in himself, in a plan of
sheer goodness freely created man to make him share in his
own blessed life. For this reason, at every time and in every
place, God draws close to man. He calls man to seek him,
to know him, to love him with all his strength.
—THE CATECHISM OF THE CATHOLIC CHURCH (FIRST THREE SENTENCES)

Dr. Thomas Hora (1914–1995) was a pathbreaking psychiatrist who taught that problems are psychological and that solutions are spiritual. His core principle was the Genesis revelation that man is "made in the image and likeness of God." He called his approach to health and healing Existential Metapsychiatry. Much of it is based on the words of Jesus. I was a student of Dr. Hora at the New York Institute of Metapsychiatry for three years. He wasn't religious, but his insights not only enriched my life but also shed light on much of "the good stuff" in my religion that has been forgotten, neglected, or ignored for too long. As my friend theologian Jack Shea once remarked, "We Catholics take help from wherever we can find it!" Dr. Hora once said that there are three kinds of people:

✛ those who are here for themselves
✛ those who are here for others
✛ those who are here for God

The first "mode of being in the world" is self-confirmatory and leads to self-destruction. The second is the flip side of the first; when we do good to feel good we also get in trouble. The third—to be here for God—is the key to eternal life. How similar to the teachings quoted from the two Catholic catechisms above!

When we are here for God—when we endeavor to know, love, and serve him in this world—we not only share in God's own blessed life but also begin to realize happiness with him forever. Eternity begins on the spot where we are standing.

The Catechism of the Catholic Church opens with this epigraph: "This is eternal life, that they may know you, the only true God, and Jesus Christ, whom you have sent" (John 17:3). That same epigraph is on the very first page of Dr. Hora's book *Dialogues in Metapsychiatry*, and underneath it: "The meaning and purpose of life is to come to know Reality."

When we come to know God who is Love and in whose image we are made, and Jesus Christ whom Love has sent as a light into the world (John 8:12), we cannot help but choose to be here for God, and to love and serve him because we see that God's will for us is more wonderful than anything we can imagine.

God doesn't want to hurt us. His will for us is good, pleasing and perfect (Romans 12:2). We hurt when we forget or ignore Reality: what and where we really are—likenesses of Love who live and move and have our being in Love. The key is to know it and to show it. The church teaches that we suffer when we disobey the will of God. Dr. Hora put it this way: "We suffer from what we want and what we don't want." When we don't want what Love wants, trouble is sure to follow. Isn't it helpful to read about the same truths in different words?

What does God want? God wants us to know we're in Love. Jesus asks us to be that love in the world. "Love one another as I have loved you" (John 15:12). That's all we need to study, that's all we need to know. It's the beginning of eternal life. "God is love. Whoever lives in love lives in God, and God in him" (1 John 4:16, NIV).

> God is love. On this solid rock the entire faith of the Church is based.
> —POPE BENEDICT XVI

So why do bad things happen to good people? What's up with that?

I don't know. And neither does anybody else.

You won't find me saying Catholicism has the final word on that question. Indeed, to its credit, the church has always said it is a mystery. Like you and everyone else I've been wrestling with that question my whole life. I've talked with friends about it over kitchen tables. I've read the works of Catholic saints and Zen sages and Indian seers. Like anybody else, when it comes to pain, loss, and depression, I look for help wherever I can find it. As a publisher I've asked many Catholic authors whose insights I appreciate to write books on suffering just so I could read what they discovered and pass it along to others. When it comes to the question, why do bad things happen to good people, Dr. Hora gave me a good lead. Any question beginning with "Why?" he said, is futile. When you start asking why, you become like a snake chasing its own tail. You get dizzy with follow-up questions that go nowhere, like "Who's to blame? How do I feel? What's wrong? What should I do? How should I do it? What shouldn't I do? Why shouldn't I do it? Why am I going nuts?!" That's not spiritual inquiry; that's cable news talk. The question, "Why did God make you?" is really "What is your purpose in life?" Questions beginning with "What?" are helpful. "If we know what," Dr. Hora wrote, "then we know how."

So then, what is the meaning of suffering? What's it all about, Alfie? The 928-page *Catechism* has only one listing for "Suffering" in its 107-page index, and that refers to a brief paragraph on the

> *Not everything is immediately good to those who seek God, but everything is capable of becoming good.*
> —Teilhard de Chardin,
> *The Divine Milieu*

suffering of Christ. What can we learn from the spiritual deposit of faith?

Mother Teresa tells the story of consoling a little girl who was sick and in pain. She told the child, "You should be happy that God sends you suffering because your sufferings are proof that God loves you very much. Your sufferings are kisses from Jesus."

"Then, Mother," said the girl, "please ask Jesus not to kiss me so much."

Mother Teresa got the joke on herself. Suffering is not a good. When we tell someone that we're hurting and they, in sincerity, say to us, "Don't worry. God never sends us more than we can handle," be polite, but remember the Mother Teresa story. The philosopher Ludwig Wittgenstein observed, "What can be said at all can be said clearly, and whereof what one cannot speak, thereon one must be silent." Fr. Matt Hoffman, my freshman English teacher in high school, a teddy bear of a man, told us the best response to someone at a funeral parlor or in a hospital is a hug. A real one.

"God had one son on earth without sin," wrote Augustine, "but never one without suffering." Dr. Hora used to say that "suffering isn't necessary, but it is inevitable." I say, nobody gets out of this thing alive. Robert Ellsberg writes in *The Saints' Guide to Happiness*:

> The saints do not teach us how to avoid suffering; they teach us how to suffer. They do not provide the "meaning" of suffering. But they lived by the assurance

that there is a meaning or truth *at the heart of life* that suffering is powerless to destroy. They did not believe that suffering is good but that God is good and that "neither death nor life, nor height nor depth" can deprive us of access to that good if we truly desire it. They found that there is no place that is literally "god-forsaken," but that in every situation, even the most grim and painful, there is a door that leads to love, to fullness of life, to happiness. This is the deepest mystery of the gospel. Our task, if we would learn from the saints, is to find that door and enter in.

Of all the authors I've asked to write a book about suffering, the one who moved me the most is Fr. William O'Malley, SJ, in *Redemptive Suffering*. A high school teacher of religion and English for almost fifty years, Bill knows how to talk to kids. And that's the kind of language I need when shivering in awe at the magnitude of the mystery of evil. Like the priest I wrote about in chapter 4, whose every sermon was on the love of Jesus, Bill draws readers to Jesus on the cross as our exemplar. He tells a story that stuns us with its simplicity:

One time during Easter week, a frighteningly intelligent little boy named Cisco, who had gone to all the Holy Week ceremonies, asked me, "Father, if God really loved his Son so much, why would he ask him to go through such an awful, awful death?" My only answer to him then is my only answer to him now: To show us how it's done. With dignity.

Bill O'Malley lives what he teaches. He's one of those guys whose face is a road map of suffering and joy. He can wince and smile at the same time. If you saw the movie *The Exorcist*, Bill was the

> The Son of God suffered unto the death, not that men might not suffer, but that their sufferings might be like his.
> —GEORGE MACDONALD

kindly priest at the end of the movie whom Linda Blair, no longer possessed, runs up to and hugs. That's the kind of guy he is.

The mystery of a God who is all good and a world riddled with good and evil is just that: a riddle. Andrew Greeley writes eloquently about a God who suffers with us. Others speculate that God knows nothing about suffering but is a power we can tap into to help carry our cross. Richard Rohr sheds practical light in *Job and the Mystery of Suffering*:

> The human question when we are hanging on our cross is first, "Why is my life like this?" (We all probably start there.) But grace leads us to an amazing and startling recognition, "My life is not about me." Think about that for the rest of your years. My life is not about me—this is the great and saving revelation that comes only from the whirlwind, and we are never ready for it.
>
> It helps to remember that our suffering is not just for ourselves and not just about ourselves. Joyfully borne, suffering also helps other people. Redemptive suffering is, I believe, a radical call to a deeper life and deeper

faith that affects not only the self but others. I visit hospitals and see people suffering with resignation and even joy. Afterward, I feel my energy quadrupled. That's no small thing—the life we can share with others when we unite in the spirit of Christ's crucifixion and resurrection.

Every October I travel to St. Mary of the Lake Seminary in Mundelein, Illinois, for a two-day retreat with twenty of my classmates from 1966. Each year four of us volunteer to give a brief presentation to stimulate discussion and prayer. We sit in a circle in a classroom with tall windows letting in light. A few years ago I chose to talk about suffering simply because it's a topic I think about a lot. I don't remember what I said, but I was as sincere as the simple priest who always talks about Jesus. At the end of the presentation Tom Smith said, "Thank you. I have to talk about something." He told us about his beloved daughter who had recently committed suicide. He talked for ten minutes. He was sitting on a wooden desk-chair that was like a cross holding him down, but he gave us his wounded heart, and at just the right moment Johnny Pritcher stood up and said, "All right, guys, group hug!" We all rose and embraced, and tears flowed, and love passed from one guy to another to the whole world.

That was a moment when I understood something about suffering and the overwhelming love of God. I stay Catholic because of the love of God that comes through friends.

6

The Mystics, or There's a Way of Knowing That Has Nothing to Do with the Brain

In the days ahead you will either be a mystic (one who has experienced God for real) or nothing at all.
—KARL RAHNER

There's a big difference between knowing God and knowing *about* God. Words about God are not God. The words we read in this or any other book are not "the truth that sets us free" (John 8:32). The Zen master says, "The finger pointing in the direction of the moon is not the moon." The scientist Alfred Korzybski reminds us, "The map is not the territory." *A Course in Miracles* says, "Words are symbols of symbols and thus twice removed from reality." *The Catechism of the Catholic Church* says, "We do not believe in formulas but in the realities they express." And Jesus says, "God is Spirit, and they that worship him must worship him in spirit and in truth" (John 4:24).

Words change. Maps amend. Formulas revise. And catechisms come and go. But the chosen part of things, that which lasts, which is spiritual, remains forever. Catholicism is not knowing about God but coming to know God.

How do we do that?

We can start by paying attention to what spiritual masters have to say. Theologian Karl Rahner, SJ (1904–1984), widely acknowledged as "the Thomas Aquinas of the twentieth century," wrote in *Encounters with Silence*:

> Thanks to your mercy, O Infinite God, I know something about you not only through concepts and words, but through experience. I have actually *known you* through living contact. I have *met you* in joy and suffering. For you are the first and last experience of my life. Yes, really you yourself, not just a concept of you, not just the name which we ourselves have given to you! You have descended upon me in water and the Spirit, in my baptism. And then there was no question of my convincing or excogitating anything about you. Then my reason with its extravagant cleverness was still silent. Then, without asking me, you made yourself my poor heart's destiny.

That's awesome. There's a way of knowing God that has nothing to do with formulas, concepts, or even words. Ironically, the title for this chapter was inspired by my favorite atheist, Woody Allen. In his movie *Manhattan*, he says to Diane Keaton, "The brain is the most overrated organ. There's a way of knowing that has nothing to do with the brain." The Zen masters speak about direct knowing. The Catholic mystics speak about direct consciousness of the awareness of God. Bernard McGinn in his magisterial three-volume work *The Presence of God: A History of Western Christian Mysticism* writes:

> The ways in which this special form of encounter with God have been understood are multiple. One thing that all Christian mystics have agreed on is that the experience in itself defies conceptualization and verbalization, in part or in whole."

St. Teresa of Ávila (1515–1582), the great mystical doctor of the church, described "a consciousness of the presence of God of such a kind that I could not possibly doubt that God was within me and I was totally engulfed in him." St. Teresa, by the way, was the author of this famous spiritual quote:

> Christ has no body on earth but yours; no hands, no feet on earth but yours. Yours are the eyes with which he looks compassionately on this world. Yours are the feet with which he walks to do good. Yours are the hands with which he blesses all the world. Christ has no body now on earth but yours.

You're familiar with it because you have seen it on T-shirts, tote bags, mugs, and mouse pads. Who says people today aren't interested in being mystics?

The mystical experience is characterized by a sense of oneness. Our eyes are Christ's eyes beholding the world.

It's impossible to define. But imagine a sunbeam being suddenly aware that it is one with the sun and all the other rays of the sun. It knows no separation. Or imagine a wave conscious of its oneness with the ocean and all the other waves. In truth, there is no sun or sunbeam. There is only light. There are no waves. There is only water. That is direct knowing. It is non-knowing.

That's about the best I can do.

So let me tell you a story. Again it involves Dr. Thomas Hora, who was not Catholic but who unlocked the spiritual wisdom in my faith with extraordinary grace.

I was leaving his office on West 72 Street near Central Park on a bright October afternoon. He had said to me, "You are God's special child." Nothing I had not heard many times since first grade at St. Andrew's, but it stuck this time. I remember standing on the corner of Central Park West, waiting for a bus, and suddenly, without my willing it, the words disappeared, and I *knew*. I stood there, not moving, and it was like the world wasn't moving either, but it was, at just the right speed. It was a sunny day, and you could trace the veins on the leaves of trees a block away and feel the warm breeze and hear the silence amidst the buzz of the street. I looked at the people walking on this side and that, strolling in the park with their dogs or sitting on a bench with their books and it was a moment like Thomas Merton must have experienced as he stood on a street corner in Louisville, Kentucky, and thought, *"There is no way of telling people that they are all walking around shining like the sun!* It was one of those moments when all the planets and all the buses and all the people and all the squirrels are just where they are supposed to be. It was like that long-ago afternoon when a softball floated like a butterfly into my hands on a side street near Wrigley Field. Like the day I saw Christ on Clark Street, drinking whiskey from a bottle in a paper bag. Is this what St. Teresa was talking about? Is this what mysticism is about?

> *The eye with which I see God is the same eye with which God sees me.*
> —MEISTER ECKHART
>
> *Then I saw a new heaven and a new earth; for the first heaven and the first earth had passed away.*
> —REVELATION 21:1, NRSV

Seeing the everyday world with eyes not ours?

Have you had an experience like that? I bet you have. It doesn't last long, but you remember it. And its promise keeps you going.

The finger pointing in the direction of the moon is not the moon, but it's helpful to have spiritual directors—people or icons or a Bible or a spiritual book—to point us in the right direction. I have always found spiritual reading the best trigger for letting go and letting God. This practice is part of an ancient Catholic tradition called *lectio divina*, or holy reading. Have you ever been reading a spiritual book and suddenly the mind stands still, the book falls, and you know what the psalmist meant: "Be still, and know that I am God!" (Psalm 46:10, NRSV) Every now and then it helps to be given a finger.

Moments of awareness when we are conscious of the presence of God don't come often to anyone. As we learned in chapter 3, God comes when we least expect him. It's all about God, not us. What we can do is be interested in God and the things of God and . . . maybe . . . sometime . . . without notice . . . *an Easter moment*! I don't know a better way to put it. And it's one big reason, since Catholicism is the *locus* where my interest was first sparked, that I am Catholic still.

7

The Mystical Body of Christ

No man is an island, entire of itself; every man is a piece
of the continent, a part of the main. . . . Any man's death
diminishes me, because I am involved in mankind.
—JOHN DONNE, *DEVOTIONS UPON EMERGENT OCCASIONS*

If one part of the body suffers, every part suffers with it.
If one part is honored, every part rejoices with it.
—1 CORINTHIANS 12:26

We were eating brunch at our favorite diner. Vickie asked me what I was going to work on when we got home. "Chapter 7," I said, "The Mystical Body. It's a tough one."

"Can I help you?" she asked.

"Sure," I answered. "What do you think the Mystical Body of Christ is?"

She picked up a French fry and held it to the side of her head as if it were a quill and she was poised to write. "Well, "she said, "we're all part of one body, and Christ is here to help us."

"That's it, "I said, "except a lot of people think it refers only to Catholics."

She bit into her French fry. "That can't be."

"Why not?"

"Because Christ died for all of us."

"Thanks," I said. "You just helped me."

Pope Pius XII popularized the phrase Mystical Body of Christ in his 1943 encyclical *Mystici Corporis Christi*. He described the church as a mystical union of all Christians with Jesus as their head. Twenty-two years later the Second Vatican Council gave the world *Lumen Gentium*, or *Light of the World*, a historic document that expanded the term to include, at least potentially, everybody of all time because . . . well . . . Christ died for all of us.

Still, many Catholics to this day think that this beautiful phrase points not to the moon but to a satellite. When Therese Borchard and I wrote our book, *I Like Being Catholic*, we wrote to hundreds of Catholics, famous and ordinary like us. The late, great Cardinal O'Connor of New York wrote back, "The most amazing thing to me about being Catholic is that I am able to unite myself in faith with men and women not only throughout the world but throughout the centuries." John O'Connor didn't think in a box. Like Vickie, he knew: Jesus came for all of us, the living, the dead, and those to come. For God there is no BC and AD. There is only now.

We can, however, trace the literary DNA of this concept to the corpus of letters written by St. Paul in the first century:

Just as the body is one and has many members, and all the members of the body, though many, are one body, so it is with Christ. (1 Corinthians 12:12, NRSV)

We were all baptized by one Spirit into one body—whether Jews or Greeks, slave or free—and we were all given the one Spirit to drink. Now the body is not made up of one part but of many. (1 Corinthians 12:13–14, NIV)

And so it is. We are all baptized—whether by water or desire—into one *Spirit,* given one *Spirit* to drink, are indeed *one spiritual body!* Talk about the chosen part of things! There is nothing in this idea that imprisons us in bodies of flesh that break and get sick and turn to dust. No one can restrict membership to the Mystical Body of Christ as if it were some kind of religious country club. We are *all* members of one spiritual body! Mystical means "of a spiritual nature." It wasn't Oprah who famously said, "We are not human beings having a spiritual experience; we are spiritual beings having a human experience." It was Teilhard de Chardin (*The Phenomenon of Man,* 1955), the Catholic paleontologist who spent his life looking at rocks and seeing eternity. Remember reading in the last chapter that "God is Spirit, and those who worship him must

> We are already one. But we imagine that we are not. And what we have to recover is our original unity. What we have to be is what we are.
> —Thomas Merton, speech in Calcutta, 1968

worship in spirit and truth" (John 4:24, NRSV)? That's what it's all about!

When I was studying philosophy in seminary way back when, Fr. John "Spanky" McFarland, SJ, wrote on the blackboard: "You are an *unum per se!*" He wrote it so hard the chalk broke and splintered into pieces, like the beginning of a universe. He wanted us to know: this is important! Spanky was a great teacher but never fully explained what he meant by *unum per se*. It was one of those truths he wanted us to *see*.

The philosopher Gottfried Wilhelm Leibniz (1646–1716) coined those words. His name reminds me of a Mel Brooks character out of *Young Frankenstein* but in fact, Leibniz was one of the great minds of the seventeenth century and used the controversial term *unum per se* to describe the remarkable unity of body, mind, and soul. Three hundred years later we pick up magazines with names like *Body, Mind, and Spirit* on coffee tables in our doctors' offices.

While Fr. McFarland never fully explained *unum per se*, our English teacher Fr. Burrill pointed us in the right direction. He taught us Catholic poetry. He taught us Gerard Manley Hopkins, who taught us all that each of us

Acts in God's eye what in God's eye he is—
Christ—for Christ plays in ten thousand places,
Lovely in limbs, and lovely in eyes not his
To the Father through the features of men's faces.

Not only is the hand bone connected to the neck bone and the neck bone connected to the brain and the brain to the mind and the mind to the soul—all one—but I am part of you and you are part of me and we are all one in Christ. I wouldn't put it that way to a Jewish or Muslim or Buddhist friend but they, too, *see* the chosen part of things.

The New Physics also points us in the direction of the moon and sheds light on the Mystical Body of Christ. It demonstrates that there is, in fact, no space between any of us. It talks about "the butterfly effect," how when a butterfly flaps its wings in India a storm can brew in Indiana. What happens to each of us happens to all of us. When a child in Calcutta goes hungry, a child in California can sense her pain. When a Samaritan helps a wounded man on the side of the road, a hospital goes up two thousand years later. What blesses one blesses all. All at once and forever! The Mystical Body of Christ is not an institution; it is a reality. That's why I stay in the church: so I can talk with people about it from the place I first learned about it. Right here, right now.

> Hear, O Israel, Adonai is our God, Adonai is One!
> —DEUTERONOMY 6:4

> There is nothing but God. God is the Light of the heavens and the earth.
> —THE QUR'AN

> One perfect nature pervades and circulates within all natures. One all-inclusive Reality contains and embraces all realities. One moon is reflected in every expanse of water. Every reflected moon is one moon. The essence of all Buddhas is in my being. My essence is in their being.
> —YUNG-CHIA TA-SHIH, ZEN MASTER

8

The Communion of Saints

To be connected with the Church is to be associated with
scoundrels, warmongers, fakes, child-molesters, murderers,
adulterers and hypocrites of every description. It also, at the
same time, identifies you with saints and the finest persons
of heroic soul within every time, country, race, and gender.
To be a member of the church is to carry the mantle of both
the worst sin and the finest heroism of soul because the
church always looks exactly as it looked at the
original crucifixion, God hung among thieves.
—Ronald Rolheiser, *The Holy Longing*

And one of those thieves won a ticket to heaven. I love
saints. Not the plaster saints who can do no wrong, but
the real ones who are both larger than life and just like us.

✛ St. Joseph, who no doubt hit the ceiling when his newly
betrothed told him she was pregnant but who valued
fidelity so much that he married her anyway and taught
their Son to carve beauty from beams of wood.

✛ Mary, the mother of Jesus, who emptied herself of ego so she could be filled with the light of the world, who laughed with her toddler, scolded her adult son when he refused to turn water into wine at a wedding feast (he did it her way), and cried as she held him in her arms at the foot of his cross.

✛ Mary Magdalene, the public sinner who washed Jesus' feet with her tears and dried them with her hair, who Jesus lifted and said, "Her sins are forgiven because she loves much" (Luke 7:46). If Mary Magdalene was not at Jesus' side during the Last Supper, you can bet she was one of the women who prepared it. It was she among all the disciples who did not desert Jesus when he was arrested and crucified, and it was she to whom Jesus chose to appear first when he walked out of the tomb.

✛ Hildegard of Bingen (1098–1179), who like so many nuns today could do it all: teach, write, paint, cook, compose music, make medicine, found a religious community, communicate with peasants and kings, and get in hot water from a bishop for burying a sinner in her abbey's cemetery.

✛ Thomas Aquinas (1225–1274), a theologian who ate too much, whom fellow students called a "Dumb Ox," and who wrote the *Summa Theologiae*, which shaped the history of Catholic thought. Now a doctor of the church, Aquinas got into trouble in his day, too, for mining wisdom from the philosophy of a pagan (Aristotle), and for developing a system of thought that did not rely on church authority but on looking at diverse points of view and letting the truth speak its own name. Heard that one before?

✛ St. Bonaventure (1221–1274), a classmate of Aquinas who was as different from his friend as Mr. Wizard is from Stephen Hawking. Bonaventure was a mystic who wrote some of the most profound books in the treasury of Catholicism. Wouldn't you like to hear the conversations he and Aquinas had as they walked along the Seine with their schoolbooks, on their way to the University of Paris? Bonaventure was also named a doctor of the church and is known as the Seraphic Doctor because he was an angel. Did I forget to tell you that Bonaventure is my favorite saint and that I sign off many of my e-mails with "Buona Ventura," which means "Good Luck"?

✛ Brother Lawrence (1611–1691), an ordinary guy who spent forty years cooking hot meals in a monastery kitchen but made such an impression on his peers that his few words of wisdom are memorialized in *Practice of the Presence of God*. "God regards not the greatness of the work," he observed, "but the love with which it is performed."

✛ St. Alphonsus Ligouri (1696–1787) who lived to be ninety-one, and that's a miracle because he suffered from a scrupulous conscience. A scrupulous conscience is a religious form of obsessive-compulsive disorder in which you can't stop thinking about your sins and imperfections and feel weighed down with guilt. It is a side effect of Catholicism poorly taught and is familiar to many Catholics of my generation. Alphonsus was afflicted with "a thousand frightening fantasies" and spent much of his life developing a spirituality to help others like him. What I love about Alphonsus is that in spite of his mental anguish, he could found the Redemptorist order, become a bishop, write more than one hundred books on theology and spirituality that have been translated into seventy-one languages, and is a model of hope. If you suffer or know someone who suffers from a scrupulous conscience, may I recommend a book called *A Thousand Frightening Fantasies* by Catholic psychologist William Van Ornum. It has a foreword by John Cardinal O'Connor and is one of the most helpful books I've had the buona fortuna to publish.

✢ St. Thérèse of Lisieux (1873–1897), who dedicated every moment of her life to relieving the suffering of others in the Mystical Body of Christ. Like Alphonsus, she sometimes tried too hard and, regrettably, spent a long time dying at an early age of tuberculosis, coughing up blood, in constant pain and near despair. But she died feeling the embrace of God's love. During her life Thérèse was a model of kindness to her fellow Sisters, not a few of them tough to live with. She thought of herself as a Little Flower and called her spiritual path the Little Way. "I am only a very little soul," she wrote, "who can only offer very little things to our Lord." Her autobiography *The Story of a Soul* remains a big thing to many readers after one hundred years in print.

These saints all have imperfections. And they are all worth imitating.

Robert Ellsberg, in his magisterial work *All Saints*, writes about saints like these who have been canonized by the church and about others who are equally deserving. "The church makes no pretense," he writes, "that its canon exhausts the number of actual saints. There are countless men and women whose holiness is recognized by God alone. Along with the 'official saints' they are commemorated by the church on November 1, the feast of All Saints." In his 365 reflections on saints, prophets, and witnesses for our time, Robert includes these contemporary heroes:

+ Mohandas Gandhi (1869–1948), the "Great Soul" of India who believed that "an eye for an eye makes the whole world blind" and taught the world to see that nonviolence is the way to peace. "It is not he who says, 'Lord, Lord' that is a Christian," he wrote, "but 'he who does the will of the Lord'—that is a true Christian."

+ Oscar Romero (1917–1980), the archbishop of San Salvador, who comforted the afflicted and afflicted the comfortable with the gospel of Jesus, and in so doing, became the first bishop martyred on the altar since Thomas Becket in 1170. "I am bound, as a pastor," he said, two weeks before his death, "by divine command to give my life for those whom I love, and that is all Salvadorans, even those who are going to kill me."

+ Oskar Schindler (1908–1974), the "Righteous Gentile," who escaped his own history by helping more than a thousand Jews escape death during the Holocaust. Nobody knows exactly why Schindler did what he did, but in the movie *Schindler's List,* the Jewish prisoner Itzhak Stern, played by Ben Kingsley, says to Schindler: "This list . . . is an absolute good. The list is life!"

✛ Flannery O'Connor (1925–1964), the bespectacled novelist from Georgia who illuminated glimmers of grace in human darkness. "I write the way I do," she wrote, "*because* (not though) I am a Catholic," and "The only thing that makes the church endurable is that it is somehow the Body of Christ and that on this we are fed."

✛ Mother Teresa of Calcutta (1910–1997) whom critics mocked when she wrote about losing her faith, and who was a saint precisely because she despaired yet still went on. "If you judge people," she once said, "you have no time to love them."

✛ Cardinal Joseph Bernardin (1928–1996), the archbishop of Chicago who presented us with "the seamless garment of life," the understanding that all life, from womb to tomb, is sacred, and who forgave the young man who tried to destroy his life with a false accusation of molestation. "We cannot run away from our family," Bernardin said. "We have only one family, so we must make every effort to be reconciled."

Many of us Catholics stay in the church because it has introduced us to people like these who are larger than life but just like us.

> *The saints are the sinners who keep on trying.*
> —ROBERT LOUIS STEVENSON

When Therese Borchard and I were writing our book, *I Like Being Catholic*, we wrote to hundreds of people. One of the many responses that didn't make it into the book was this one from our friend Tom Bruce. As the Bible says: "Now is the acceptable time" (2 Corinthians 6:2, NRSV).

> For me personally it's the Communion of Saints. I've been working for the Franciscans for 15 years and had the opportunity to visit Assisi and Rome last year. I am always struck by the nearness of Francis, Anthony, and Clare and other Franciscan saints. This is true of Catholicism as a whole. The Catholic Church is a large dysfunctional family that we all can identify with. You may not like everything about your family but you learn to deal with them. It is the reason Catholics love saints. They are like old—or crazy—aunts and uncles we love and we have known since we were kids. There is a history of 2000 years of seeing how people in the church have tried to follow Jesus—warts and all. They are real people reflecting the culture of their times.

The communion of saints is not just about imitating and loving these folks, it's also about going to them. Listen to this cradle Catholic who knows what he's talking about:

> Catholics have saints—more than 10,000 of them. They're like God's customer service reps, and each of them has a specialty. Say you lose your wallet. You

could bother the Creator to help you find it, but if you're a Catholic, you don't have to. Just pray to St. Anthony. Finding lost things is all he does. Also there are times when you might want to pray to St. Agatha. She's the patron saint of nursing and bell-making. If you're both a nurse and a bell-maker, that's one-stop shopping. (Stephen Colbert in *I Am America*)

Still Catholic? Sure. I've got more than ten thousand reasons to still hang out.

9

There's Still Something about Mary

She is a reflection of eternal light, / a spotless mirror of the working of God, and an image of his goodness.
—WISDOM 7:26, NRSV

In her beautiful book *Mary*, the poet Kathy Coffey reminds us how often Mary must have gazed into the face of her son. Did she look into her baby's eyes and think as all mothers do, *He has my eyes*? Did his laughter ignite her joy? Did his resolve remind her of her purpose? Jesus was the mirror of God, and Mary was a mirror to her son. What she saw was a reflection of God. Isn't that how it is with mothers?

There's something about Mary that still charms us, attracts us, and makes us want to be better women and men.

In Mel Gibson's movie *The Passion of the Christ*, we see the boy Jesus fall down and Mary rush to help him, as any mother would. The movie cuts to Jesus falling under the weight of his cross, and again Mary rushes to help him, as any mother would. As a young man Jesus playfully splashes his mother with water, and they laugh and she chases him in a scene that mirrors a time from our own youth. When Jesus suffers the agony in the garden, his mother wakes from her sleep, sensing his pain as if it were her own. She follows her son on the way of the cross, wiping his blood from the ground after he is scourged, squeezing through the crowds to comfort him, and standing with the disciple John when Jesus says to them from the cross: "Woman, behold your son! Son, behold your mother!"

Catholics do not worship Mary. They honor her, imitate her, and love her—as Jesus did.

Any good mother is worthy of no less.

One should honor Mary as she herself wished and as she expressed it in the Magnificat. She praised God for his deeds. How then can we praise her? The true honor of Mary is the honor of God, the praise of God's grace. . . . Mary is nothing for the sake of herself, but for the sake of Christ. . . . Mary does not wish that we come to her, but through her to God.
—MARTIN LUTHER, EXPLANATION OF THE MAGNIFICAT, 1521

Just like everyone else, whenever we have a need, Vickie and I pray. We hold hands, and one of us takes the lead. If it's me, I talk directly to God for both of us, sort of like: "Dear God, our worries about *(fill in the blank)* are killing us. Please help us to think your thoughts, not our own. Take away our worries, and replace them with your peace. We put this problem on the altar of your love. We know you will take it from us and everything will be okay in your time, not ours. We know your will for us is better than anything we can imagine. Thy will be done. Okay, we're not going to think about this anymore. Thank you,

God." That works pretty well, even though we may have to repeat it later in the day. Now if Vickie takes the lead, we hold hands and it goes exactly like this:

> Our Father who art in heaven, hallowed be thy name. Thy kingdom come, thy will be done, on earth as it is in heaven. Give us this day our daily bread, and forgive us our trespasses as we forgive those who trespass against us. And lead us not into temptation but deliver us from evil. Amen.
>
> Hail Mary, full of grace. The Lord is with thee. Blessed art thou amongst women and blessed is the fruit of thy womb Jesus. Holy Mary, mother of God, pray for us sinners now and at the hour of our death. Amen.

And that works too. Vickie knows from experience: the best way to get to a son is through his mother.

Catholics who feel a bond with Mary know, as Martin Luther did, that when they go to God through Mary, it works. They can't prove it intellectually. They know it through the spiritual fruits that sprout from their prayer: peace, understanding, gratitude. Jesus put it this way: "You will know them by what they produce. People don't pick grapes from thorn bushes or figs from thistles, do they?" (Matthew 7:16, adapted). Catholics go to God through Mary and receive grapes, figs, apples, pears, and sometimes pizza. It works.

Mary's presence in the lives of Catholics—and anyone else who goes to God through her—is the presence of a mother. She is the beat of Jesus' heart. She is a mirror that shows us who and what we are. The mystic Meister Eckhart said it best:

> What good is it to me if Mary is full of grace and if I am not also full of grace? What good is it to me for the Creator to give birth to his Son if I do not also give birth to him in *my* time and *my* culture? . . . We are all meant to be mothers of God.

10

It's the Stories, Stupid!

Practically speaking, your religion is the
story you tell about your life.
—ANDREW GREELEY

I was eight years old and lying next to Gramma Lou on her beat-up blue sofa that smelled like my Dad. My parents were divorced, and Gramma Lou was the harbor I could always go to, to know that I was safe. Every weekday when I got off for lunch at St. Andrew's school, I'd walk through the playground to her house, where she'd make me a peanut butter-and-jelly sandwich and a cold glass of Bosco chocolate milk. After lunch we'd lie next to each other on the sofa and Gramma would read a comic book to me. Her favorite and mine was *Blackhawk*. Blackhawk was an ace fighter pilot from World War II who gathered a motley crew around him to fight injustice. Did I tell you that my dad was a WWII pilot with more missions than *Catch-22*'s Yossarian? That he earned two purple hearts and gave them to me along with his leather fly jacket that had thirty-two little bombs painted in white on the front?

He also killed Hitler with a penknife, but we won't go there, because nobody believed me then and you may not believe me now, but believe me, it's true. He told me.

That day, lying next to Gramma Lou, I pushed the comic book down with a finger and said, "Mamma Lou, I don't want to go back to school. I want to stay with you."

"We'll see," she said. "Oh, look, Chop-Chop's coming through the window!"

Chop-Chop was Blackhawk's sidekick. He used to be a cook and carried a butcher's cleaver. I pushed the comic down, turned on my side, and looked at Gramma Lou. "Momma Lou," I said, "you love me, don't you?" It was more a statement than a question.

She looked at me with her sweet brown eyes the color of Cracker Jacks. "Of course, I love you."

"Even when I'm bad, right?"

"Yes." She smiled.

"You'll always love me, won't you, Mamma Lou?"

She took me in her arms and said, "Michael, you could take Chop-Chop's hatchet and chop off my arms and chop off my legs and chop off my head and throw them all in a garbage can, and my head would still look at you and tell you again, "I love you!'"

That was the day I knew everything. Though I didn't know it at the time.

Fast forward ten years. I'm in my room at St. Mary of the Lake Seminary. No blue sofa, just a desk and a chair, a dresser and a bed. I'm reading the Gospel of John. My goal is to read the whole Bible before the end of the year. A line in the first letter of St. John stops the world. "God is love,

and he who lives in love, lives in God, and God in him."
I'm in Mamma Lou's arms again. I know for sure what my
heart knew then: God is all embracing, ever enfolding,
all knowing, ever caring, completely and unconditionally
love! God reads us comic books when we're eight years old
and unlocks the Scriptures when we grow up. Suddenly, I
had a basic premise by which to walk through life: God *is*
love. I am *in* love. Just as nothing could separate me from
the arms of Mamma Lou, nothing will ever separate me
from the love of God!

That is my Catholic story.

You don't have to be Catholic to have a story like this. You
just need a Gramma Lou. But all of my life stories seem
to have a religious dimension, and the religion I grew up
with was all about stories of God: Joseph and his pregnant
wife, Mary, fleeing to Egypt on a donkey from a mad king
who wanted to kill every boy baby in the land, and stopping in a backwater town where Mary gave birth to the
King of kings in the safety of a stable. Don Bosco gather-
ing orphans as an eagle gathers its babies under its wings,
feeding them, sheltering them, and teaching them to fly
again. Joan of Arc, a peasant girl who looked like Ingrid
Bergman and rode a horse and defeated an army, only to
be burned at the stake by a corrupt cardinal for wearing
men's clothing and listening to God's voice and refusing
to tell a lie. The stories of saints, the sagas of sinners, the
rumors of angels! Holy Thursday, Good Friday, Easter!
That's what Catholicism is about!

Does the institutional church have anything to do with all this? Sure. That's why it exists—to tell the stories.

It took four centuries for the church to chisel the doctrine of the Incarnation into a precise statement about the truth, but the story of Jesus, Mary, and Joseph was there from the beginning. Andrew Greeley writes: "It is the story that appeals to the total human. It is the beauty of the story which holds Catholics to their heritage. I'm still a Catholic because of the beauty of the Catholic stories. So are most of us Catholics. Beauty is not opposed to truth. It is simply truth in its most attractive form."

Vickie and I were having pizza the other night with our friends John and Mary Jane Cooke. They asked me what I was writing these days, and I told them I was working on a book about staying Catholic and was on the chapter called "It's the Stories, Stupid!" Mary Jane, a cradle Catholic from Buffalo, got it right away. "You know," she said, "I don't go to church anymore, but I'll always be Catholic. When I had my radiation therapy, I said the rosary every night. It was the stories—the sorrowful mysteries, the joyful mysteries—that helped me get through it. I remember making the stations of the cross when I was a little girl. I loved walking through those stories of Jesus carrying his cross, Veronica wiping his face with her veil, Simon the stranger who helped him when he fell. They're so sad and so hopeful at the same time. I loved reading stories of the saints." There was no stopping her now. "There's such comfort in hearing a story again and again," she said. "Something that doesn't change. Something that makes sense. That's why kids say, 'Tell it to me again. I want to hear it again!' The catechisms told us that Jesus loves us. The stories make it so."

And so it is.

John Shea wrote a book called *Stories of God*. In it he claims that all of us are the stories that God tells himself. And isn't it wonderful that when we go off on the wrong path, God can write straight with crooked lines? Our stories are never over. That's why I stay Catholic—to see what happens next!

11

Jesus Died for Our Sins and Rose from the Dead—*Really!*

Jesus came above all to teach us love.
—POPE JOHN PAUL II, ATTRIBUTED

If I weren't Catholic, I'd still be drawn to Jesus. Anyone who points to the birds of the air and says to his friends, "Don't worry. Look at the sparrows. They don't gather their food into barns. Your heavenly Father takes care of them. Aren't you just as valuable?"—has my attention. Anyone whose only written words were scrawled in the sand and washed away by the rain but whose teachings have changed hearts for two thousand years is worthy of everyone's attention. Anyone who can forgive the brutes who crucified him because he knew that they did *not* know what they were doing makes my hair stand on end.

And yet, a stumbling block for so many people outside the church is the teaching that serves as the church's building block: Jesus died for our sins and rose from the dead. Really? What does that mean?

Get ready for a roller-coaster ride into Aladdin's castle, down corridors of spiritual wonder that the church has ignored for too long!

Why did Jesus die? Whose fault was it? What's it all about, really? Theologians have been trying to answer these questions for centuries. The one whose theology of salvation stuck was Anselm of Canterbury (1033–1109), a man of prayer whose work *Cur Deus Homo* (Why God Became Man) never became a dogma but has influenced the church's teachings about Jesus to this day.

You are familiar with his theory. Adam and Eve, the first man and woman, offended God. That original sin demanded satisfaction. That sin got transmitted to their children and to all children ever since, something like a mutant gene. God could not just forgive Adam and Eve, let alone the human race, because divine mercy of this sort, according to Anselm, "is opposed to God's justice which allows for nothing but punishment to be the return for sin." And man, any man or all men, could not make up for that sin because God is infinite and man is finite. It would take a "God-man" to atone for Adam and Eve's sin and the inherited sin of everyone who didn't choose to be born but were born anyway for millennia to come. So God sent his only Son—innocent, loving, and infinite—to be tortured and killed as a ransom for sinful humanity.

This eleventh-century theory made it all the way to *The Baltimore Catechism* in 1885: "If God forgave us without any satisfaction, His justice would not have been satisfied and we would always feel guilty." Nobody ever asked if the reason Christians feel guilty is because they have learned that their sins nailed God to the cross, and that guilt inevitably leads to more sins and more guilt. Does this theory make sense, really?

How often do we see cynical comics on TV make fun of this vengeful god who sent his only beloved son to a cruel death for all the people who never heard of him before he was born and all those who came after? It's a god who cries out, "I don't get no satisfaction!" and a god whose existence even cradle Catholics are starting to doubt.

Questions beginning with the word why (as we saw in chapter 5) often lead to other futile questions and we wind up like snakes chasing our own tail.

Terrence Rynne in his masterful book *Gandhi and Jesus: The Saving Power of Nonviolence* writes:

> The vivid, pulsing, flesh-and-blood life of Jesus of Nazareth, his thrilling words, his arresting personality, his terrible death—the whole of what he did—all turned into a cold, bloodless courtroom scene. And that is to be Good News? It is no wonder that this message of "salvation" has so little appeal or meaning to people today. It is a wonder that this version, this extended metaphor, has endured for so long.

Is it any wonder that so many Catholics, especially Catholics hurt by the church, turn away from a church that promotes this kind of God? Fr. Joseph Ratzinger, now Pope Benedict XVI, in his book *Introduction to Christianity*

(1966) wrote: "One turns away in horror from a righteousness whose sinister wrath makes the message of love incredible."

But wait! I told you we'd be going on an adventure into the deposit of faith that has been forgotten, neglected, or ignored for too long. There is another way of looking at things! St. Anselm, a holy man who sincerely sought truth, may have won a theology contest for the ages but for every first-place winner on *American Idol* or the like, there is always a Clay Aiken. Meet Athanasius (293–373), bishop of Alexandria and doctor of the church!

It was St. Athanasius who taught that Jesus Christ, the Son of God, came into the world and died for us not as a ransom but as a gift to lead all people out of the darkness of the human condition. It was Athanasius, not Shirley MacLaine, who famously said, "God became man so we could become gods." It was Athanasius whom the *Catholic Encyclopedia* calls "the greatest champion of Catholic belief on the subject of the Incarnation that the Church has ever known and [who] in his lifetime earned the characteristic title, Father of Orthodoxy, by which he has been distinguished ever since."

Athanasius lived seven centuries before Anselm, but his simple, positive, and understandable theology of salvation didn't have legs. Neither did the theory of Abelard (1079–1142), who lived in Anselm's time and taught that it was Jesus' love and example—his life, death, and resurrection—that bring us salvation. The deposit of faith fills to overflowing with the ideas of saints and thinkers who glorify love, not fear; harmony, not suffering; and encourage us to experience life eternal, starting now, by coming to know God and Jesus Christ whom he has sent (John 17:3). It is not a God *of* love, but a God who *is* love.

The *Catechism of the Catholic Church* teaches, "The Word became flesh *so that thus we might know God's love*" (italics not mine), and "The Word became flesh *to be our model of holiness*" (ditto), and "to make us *partakers of God's nature.*" What could be more compelling?

How many Catholics who have grown tired of stale old sermons based on atonement theories that not even the pope can tolerate might stay in the church if they heard more about "the good stuff" in the deposit of faith? The "stuff" of which the Bible says each of us is made: *love.*

> If Christ was not raised, then all our preaching is useless, and your trust in God is useless.
> —1 CORINTHIANS 15:14, NLT

Jesus died for our sins and rose from the dead. Really!

And what of the resurrection of Jesus? What really happened? What does it mean?

Did Jesus physically rise from the dead, or is it a myth that points to a truth? The sacramental imagination sings. You can nail love to a cross, but you can't destroy it. "Easter means you can put truth in a grave but it won't stay there" (Clarence Hall). We begin to die the moment we're born, but Jesus gives us new life the moment he dies. Jesus was the greatest spiritual teacher who ever lived. How wonderful to believe he allowed human beings who were wracked with human guilt to scapegoat him and kill him for their fearful sins, to show once and for all that God desires love not sacrifice (Hosea 6:6), and then rose from the dead, literally, as promised, to demonstrate that everything he taught was true!

But is belief enough? Doesn't belief leave room for doubt? Doesn't doubt imply a belief? Carl Jung when asked whether or not he believed in God, answered, "I don't have to believe. I *know*."

There is a way of knowing that has nothing to do with the brain. We don't look at a cardiogram to see a loving heart any more than we ask for proof that the body needs oxygen before we breathe. Neither do we need a reporter at Bethlehem or a movie of Mary Magdalene at the tomb to know that Christ is born, Christ is risen, and Christ will come again, then and now, in us. There is more to knowing than meets the eye.

"He departed from our sight," wrote Augustine, "so we might return to our heart and there find Him. For he departed, and behold, he is *here*."

I am learning to experience the Resurrection every time I fall and rise again; every time I sin and know that to God, my scarlet sins are "whiter than snow" (Psalm 51:6); every time I see a brown leaf fall from a tree and know that a new one will be born again.

Today is the day of salvation for the world. Christ is risen from the dead: arise with him. Christ has come forth from the tomb: free yourselves from the fetters of evil. The gates of hell are open and the power of death is destroyed. The old Adam is superseded, the new perfected. In Christ a new creation is coming to birth: renew yourselves! —St. Gregory of Nazianzus, Second Oration on Easter (adapted)

I am still Catholic because the life, death, and resurrection of Jesus are important to me. Are they as important as finding out who will win *Dancing with the Stars* next week? Yes, and that is saying a lot. Are they as important to me as waking up alive tomorrow morning? No, I can't say that. But I'm still here because the church is a good place for me to keep talking with friends about Jesus, even though not as much as we talk about *Dancing with the Stars*. Isn't it amazing how we take the best things in life for granted?

12

The Church Can Change—*Really*!

*To live is to change, and to be perfect
is to have changed often.*
—John Cardinal Newman

The church has changed. The church is changing. The church will change again.

Rules, rituals, and even teachings change all the time. What doesn't change is the chosen part of things, what Hopkins called "the dearest freshness deep down things." What remains the same is beauty, not representations of beauty; truth, not statements about the truth; goodness, not good deeds. The chosen part can never change because it is spiritual.

What often troubles people about the church are the things that don't matter because they are made of matter. Let me explain.

During the first century, Peter and Paul fought over the matter of circumcision. Peter was a Jew, and circumcision was part of his tradition. Paul ministered to the Gentiles and didn't want to force upon them the Jewish law. Their argument split the new church in two. Who was worthy to become a Christian—cut or uncut? Final answer! Their debate was such a big deal that historians memorialized it as the Incident at Antioch, the religious version of *Gunfight at the O.K. Corral.* Did you know that? Of course not. Are you circumcised? Who cares?

Will anyone care two thousand years from now about today's debates? Women priests? Married priests? Who knows? One thing is certain: the expression of priesthood will change by default if not by design. It's no secret: the male celibate priest is a vanishing species. God bless all the good guys—and that is most of them—for their kindness and dedication. But the form will be as different in the future as the Cathedral of Our Lady of the Angels is different from the Cathedral of Cologne, and when the rule does change (in far less than two thousand years), people will wonder what the fuss was all about. They probably won't even know there ever *was* a fuss. The form of priesthood changes. Its chosen part remains the same: service to others for the sake of the kingdom of God.

Rules change. Since "nobody knows when" until 1966, every Catholic who ate meat on Friday went to hell. Those who were born after 1966 did not. Catholics before 1966 believed that rule and its penalty would never change. Now they wonder what happened to the poor bastards who ate a hamburger before the change.

You have to have a sense of humor about the human condition. What doesn't change is the chosen part of fasting: gratitude in place of gratification.

It's not only rules that change; rituals change as well. Did you know that the church never reached a consensus on how many sacraments there are until the thirteenth century? Did you know that Mass was said in the vernacular (native languages) until the Council of Trent in 1563, when the church mandated Latin, until 1965, and then changed it again to the vernacular? Did you know that bishops banned the laity from reading missals for centuries and now are editing the language in the millions of missals they encourage the laity to read?

You have to be patient with the human condition. What doesn't change is the chosen part of liturgy: the grace in the silence between the words.

It's not only rules and rituals that can change; so can teachings. Did you know that from day one until after the Civil War, the church considered slavery morally acceptable, as long as the masters treated their slaves humanely? that Galileo was condemned in 1633 for teaching that the earth revolved around the sun, not the other way around, as the church believed, and that the poor guy wasn't let off the hook until 1992? Did you know that until the twentieth century the church taught sex in marriage to be a necessary evil for the procreation of children?

You have to forgive the human condition. What doesn't change is the chosen part of church history: the opportunity to learn and forgive.

The late, great American bishop Raymond Lucker (1927–2001) of New Ulm, Minnesota, wrote:

> In the past the church made errors and mistakes, not on essential teachings but in reformable statements of the teaching church. It is refreshing to recognize and admit this and to acknowledge that we can grow in our understanding of the message of revelation and in the expression and application of the teaching of the church, given to us by Jesus, to different times and different cultural expressions.

Bishop Lucker had a lifelong interest in learning how to understand the difference between a definitive (unchangeable) church teaching and an authoritative (not unchangeable) teaching. The Incarnation, for instance, is clearly a definitive church teaching. Celibacy of the clergy is not. The right understanding of what is changeable and what is not can lead to a choice between a familiar path and a road less traveled that "makes all the difference" in the life of the people of God. Bishop Lucker identified sixty-four church teachings that have changed throughout history and twenty-two that could change someday because they are not definitive. Those changeable church teachings include birth control, communion of the divorced and remarried, general absolution, intercommunion, and homosexuality.

The church has not only changed throughout the ages, but it has also changed more in the fifty years since Vatican II than in the first two thousand years— just like everything else in the world. The future came yesterday, and the rate of change is the blink of an eye. Today's cell phone is tomorrow's telegraph. Two or three of the authoritative (not unchangeable) teachings of the church are poised to fall like the Berlin Wall, unexpectedly but not surprisingly. Consider birth control. In 1966 a papal commission of seventy-two experts from five continents, including bishops, clergy, physicians, and married couples, after three years of study advised Pope Paul VI that artificial birth control was not intrinsically evil and that Catholic couples should be allowed to decide for themselves what methods to use. But the head of the commission, Cardinal Alfredo Ottaviani, counseled the pope that a change in this teaching would jeopardize the church's credibility. In 1968 the pope issued the encyclical *Humanae Vitae* which reiterated the church's anti-birth-control position. Immediately the church's credibility was in jeopardy. In 2011, eight out of ten Catholics are certain that artificial birth control is a blessing, not a sin. This nondefinitive teaching can change. What will not change is the chosen part of sexual intimacy in marriage: love.

The church has changed. It is changing. It will change.

After the dust settles, the gold will remain.

I value Catholicism because I cherish the chosen part of things. I stay in the church because I want to see what happens next.

13

You Can Disagree with the Church and Still Be a Good Catholic

Years ago on *Saturday Night Live* the actors Billy Crystal and Christopher Guest played Willie and Frankie, two New York pals who are always hurting themselves and sharing their woes with each other. The running line was, "I hate when that happens!"

Willie once told Frankie about the time he took a meat thermometer and shoved it into his ear as far is it would go.

"Boy, that must smart!" Frankie said

"I know! I hate when that happens!"

Then Frankie told Willie about the time he took a carrot scraper and twisted it up his nose. "I'm getting all the mucus membranes out of there, you know? And then I take one of them, uh—?

"Mentholated eucalyptus cough drops?"

"Right. And I stick it—wedge it up there, you know? I take a couple of whiffs. Boy! You feel like your head's going to explode!"

"Right. I hate when that happens!"

You know when I feel like my head is going to explode? When I'm watching a cable talk show and two Catholics are arguing about the church and one of them tells the other: "You're not Catholic! You can't say that and still be Catholic. Why don't you just join another church?" I hate when that happens!

The person who makes that statement hurts the other and by so doing hurts himself and everybody else. He's Willie sticking a pencil in his eye and encouraging Frankie to walk on tacks. Remember when we talked about the Mystical Body of Christ in chapter 7?

> There are many parts but only one body. The eye cannot say to the hand, 'I don't need you!' And the head cannot say to the feet, 'I don't need you!' On the contrary, those parts of the body that seem to be weaker are indispensable, and the parts that we think are less honorable we treat with special honor. If one part suffers, every part suffers with it. If one part is honored, every part rejoices with it. Now you are the body of Christ, and each one of you is a part of it!" (1 Corinthians 12:20–27, NIV)

We can no more remove ourselves from the body of Christ than we can separate ourselves from our own body. The calmest answer to the challenge to leave I ever heard was from Fr. Andrew Greeley years ago on *The Phil Donahue*

Show when a woman asked him, "If you disagree with the church, why don't you just leave?"

"Because I like being Catholic."

Fr. Greeley would later famously say, "Even if they throw me out, I won't go." Indeed, the only way to leave the church is to say so yourself. The church's harshest penalty, excommunication, forbids a Catholic from receiving the sacraments until he repents; it doesn't turn anyone into an unbaptized Catholic. Catholicism is in your spiritual DNA; it traces back to a pool of blood at the foot of the cross. You can't wash it off.

The Catholic response to an individual who disagrees on a nondefinitive church teaching (as we saw in chapter 11 many of the controversial ones are open to question) is to participate with them in a mutual search for clarity. We belong to one body and cannot cut off a member without hurting the whole body. "In essentials, unity," wrote John XXIII, "in doubtful matters, liberty; and in all things, charity." The essential, of course, *is* charity. Too bad that charity doesn't make for good TV.

Not surprisingly, many of these debates are really about politics, not religion. Can a governor who supports the law on *Roe v. Wade* receive communion? Can a Supreme Court justice who rules against the church's teaching on capital punishment still call himself Catholic? And what's up with the Catholic commentators who support the church's teaching on sex and in the same breath say the pope and bishops don't know what they're talking about on issues of economics and social justice? The arguments are more about being a Democrat or a Republican than being a Catholic or a heretic.

Yet how many Catholics stop being Catholic because they cannot in conscience agree with the church on issues such as birth control and get the idea that it doesn't behoove them to stay? How many other Catholics are hanging on to the ship of the church by their fingernails because they've heard that dissent is akin to mutiny? Add to that the scandals and the undernourishing sermons, and it's a wonder that most Catholics still say with Andrew Greeley, "Even if you throw me out, I'm not leaving. It's my church too!"

A Benedictine monk of fifty years, Philip Kaufman wrote a helpful book called *Why You Can Disagree and Remain a Faithful Catholic*. He first points out that a Catholic, like any intelligent human being, has a responsibility to "follow a sincerely informed conscience. That doesn't mean that we can do whatever we please. It does mean that once we have made an honest effort to determine what we should do or avoid doing, we have an obligation to act according to that conviction."

As Pope John Paul II put it in *The Splendor of Truth*: "The judgment of conscience has an imperative character: man must act in accordance with it."

Today it is easier than ever to have an informed conscience. People can not only read, but they are also more educated—and they can google. All you have to do is google "Birth Control Encyclical" or "Birth Control Catholic" or "Papal Birth Control Commission," and you'll know as much about (if not more than) that issue in less than an afternoon (and from every point of view) as your parish priest. (Sorry, guys, but you know it's true.) Your conscience will tell *you*—you won't tell it—what makes sense for you.

And then you'll be able to go on TV and discuss the church and go home knowing that no matter what anybody says, you *are* a good Catholic!

Dissent doesn't make someone an ill-informed Catholic; disinterest does.

I'm still here because these things interest me tremendously, and I'm still Catholic because I'm still learning.

14

The Bethlehem Principle (There Is Room in the Church for Everyone or There Is Room for No One)

The church is a house with 100 gates; and no
two men enter at exactly the same angle.
—G. K. CHESTERTON

Way back when, I helped write a business plan for the new Crossroad Publishing Company. Crossroad was a small religious book publisher with strong Catholic roots. As I wrote, a principle wrote itself. I called it the Bethlehem Principle. It went like this:

> There must be room in Crossroad—as there is in the church—for everyone. Two thousand years ago there was no room at the inn for a carpenter and his pregnant wife. And look who they turned out to be! To exclude anyone is to exclude everyone. To give voice to the voiceless is to raise a "shout for joy and gladness" (Psalm 35:27). To move forward is to take risks.

James Joyce famously said, "Catholicism means here comes everybody!" Crossroad means there is a place for Catholics on the left side of the road, the right side, and especially the middle where most Catholics are stumbling toward Bethlehem.

We went on to publish every pope and every theologian a pope would admonish; we made public the ideas of Cardinal Ratzinger before and during his tenure as Prefect for the Congregation of the Faith, as well as the Catholics he questioned; we published the biography of Mother Angelica and the story of Patty Crowley and her adventure on the Papal Birth Control Commission. Most of all we published everybody in-between: Henri Nouwen, Joyce Rupp, folks whose words have nourished Catholics for decades. They are all, each of them, Catholic, and each of them has words and stories that can benefit us all.

And guess what? Nobody ever kicked any of those folks out of the church. They can't.

Somehow, despite the rhetoric, we all *know*: there is room in the church for everyone, or there is room for no one.

There is room in the church for every pope and for everyone he corrects and for everyone who corrects him; for members of Call to Action and followers of Opus Dei; for those who receive communion on the pillow of their tongue and for those who prefer the cup of their palm; for those who save their money for a pilgrimage to Medjugorje and for those who blow it at Vegas; for sinners, saints, and fools.

Too many Catholics fall away from the church because they think there is no room for them. Now more than ever the church must shout out that there *is* room in the inn for everyone. This is not merely a publishing principle— it's the way it is!

Most of all, the church must make space for those it has hurt. "In my Father's house," Jesus said, "there are many dwelling places" (John 14:2, NRSV). Would not Jesus, if he were here today, prepare a great room, a family room of enormous comfort, for victims of abuse, for gay and lesbian Catholics, for divorcees, and for Catholic thinkers who seek to shed light but too often receive only heat in return? If there is not room for everyone, the church is not a home but a country club.

Thomas Merton wrote in *Raids on the Unspeakable*: "[Christ's] place is with those who do not belong, who are rejected by power because they are regarded as weak, those who are discredited, who are denied the status of persons. . . . In these He hides Himself, for whom there is no room."

What the church finds when it follows the example of Jesus is that those who have the biggest wounds are the biggest lovers. Listen to Italian writer Carlo Carretto (1910–1988):

> How much I must criticize you, my church, and yet how much I love you! You have made me suffer more than anyone, and yet I owe more to you than to anyone. I should like to see you destroyed, and yet I need

your presence. You have given me much scandal, and yet alone have made me understand holiness.

Never in this world have I seen anything more compromised, more false, yet never have I touched anything more pure, more generous, or more beautiful. Countless times I have felt like leaving you, my church; and yet every night I have prayed that I might die in your warm, loving arms!

Jesus calls us all to a great feast whose tables are set for everyone: "the poor, the crippled, the blind, and the lame"—and there is still room for more! (Luke 14:15–24).

Catholicism means throwing a party for everyone. We need someone to remind us that the church is a family. Dissent doesn't break up families; disinterest does.

The church as family fills its table to bursting for prodigal sons and daughters—morning, noon, and night. Like the parent in that parable, such a church refuses to condemn or even compare one family member to another. It takes Jesus' word to heart: "Do not judge, and you will not be judged. Do not condemn, and you will not be condemned. Forgive, and you will be forgiven" (Luke 6:36–38, NIV). Or better yet, "My child, you are always with me, and everything I have is yours!" (Luke 15:31, adapted)

I am still Catholic because the story of Bethlehem teaches me we are all welcome. I stay in the church because I know this is true no matter what anybody says.

15

A Dizzying Array of Images
for the Church

*Understanding means seeing that the same thing
said different ways is the same thing.*
—LUDWIG WITTGENSTEIN

So what is the Catholic Church anyway? Is it the same as
Catholicism? What does the church think it is? What do
you mean by *it?*

The church has defined itself over the centuries as the
Mystical Body of Christ (my favorite), the bride of Christ,
the family of God, the people of God, the temple of the
Holy Spirit, and many other beautiful metaphors founded
on a spiritual reality.

There are many ways to define the same word. Just as
we call the United States a country, a community, a bea-
con, a pioneer, and a protector, we can define the church
as an institution, a mystical communion, a sacrament, a
herald, and a servant. What a dizzying array of images!
Every metaphor points to a chosen part of Catholicism.

I first knew church as a redbrick building with twin spires on the corner of Addison and Paulina streets in Chicago. I soon knew it as St. Andrew's parish. It was the place where I first learned about Jesus. I also learned how to fight and how to get out of fighting, but maybe that's another story. What made St. Andrew's *church* was not that its spires pointed to heaven but that its flawed people— priests, sisters, parishioners—embodied the mystery of the metaphors: mystical body, family of God, sacrament, servant. Poised between heaven and earth where the visible reaches for the invisible, St. Andrew's was at once a scary place and a sacred place. It was a place on earth where blades of grass could break through cracks in the pavement. Without its spiritual foundation St. Andrew's would be just a pile of bricks. With it, it was a place where we could begin to learn that we are not alone but are members of God's family.

Later in life I would learn through the study of meta-psychiatry that each of us is a "place" where God reveals himself. Having learned in seminary that God is unconditional love, I could put one and one together and understand that my purpose in life is to be a place where love reveals itself. I could also now see how two and two equal church: a place where God reveals himself through members of a community learning to love one another as Jesus did. "Where two or three are gathered in my name, I am there among them" (Matthew 18:20, NRSV).

The Catholic Church is St. Andrew's parish. Only bigger.

Martin Sheen is an actor by profession, but he speaks the wisdom of a theologian. The church is a spiritual community learning to see with Jesus' eyes. Jesus asks the members of his mystical body to participate in God's mission of love and forgiveness.

> *It doesn't really matter how much of the rules or the dogma we have accepted and live by if we're not really living by the fundamental creed of the Catholic Church, which is service to others and finding God in ourselves and then seeing God in everyone— including our enemies.*
> —MARTIN SHEEN

The church is all about beholding God's presence and action and spreading God's reign that began before the beginning and will have no end.

A wonderful old Maryknoll priest, John Walsh, likes to say, "Church doesn't have a mission. Mission has a church." Pope Benedict XVI has often said, "The church talks too much about structures and not enough about God." God's mission is to turn the world inside out so that we can see the kingdom that is within us (Luke 17:21) and manifest it in our lives. It is a spiritual kingdom of love, reconciliation, and healing.

We don't have to trek across the Himalayas or take a boat down the Amazon or jeep through Africa to extend God's kingdom to all nations (Matthew 28:19). We can do mission by *being* mission on the spot where we are standing. The kingdom of God is spiritual, and so it has no boundaries. It spreads from one corner of the earth to the other "in the twinkling of an eye" (1 Corinthians 15:52).

An eager friar told St. Francis that he couldn't wait to leave the cloister and spread the gospel to the world. Francis smiled and said, "We must preach the good news at all times. If necessary, we use words."

The mission is our everyday lives.

Catholic missiologist Stephen Bevans, SVD, teaches that we are most church not when we are putting mortar on bricks or adding members to a roster but when we are outside of church: "being good parents, being loving spouses, being diligent and honest in our workplace, treating our patients with care if we are health workers, going the extra mile with our students if we are teachers, living lives responsible to the environment, being responsible citizens, sharing our resources with the needy, standing up for social justice, treating immigrants fairly, trying to understand people of other faiths."

We learn, too, that just as we don't have to be Jewish to believe in one God, we don't have to be Catholic to manifest the kingdom of God. The Muslim in Morocco, the Buddhist in Kyoto, the Christian in Kenya are not rivals but allies, companions, and friends on our common journey home. Clement of Alexandria wrote in the first century: "There is but one river of truth, but many streams pour into it from this side and from that." *The Catechism of the Catholic Church* in the twentieth century teaches that "all religions bear witness to men's essential search for God." Religions are different, but God's mission is one. All of us "live and move and have our being in God," and the purpose of life is to come to see that truth so that our lives, not our religions, can be in harmony.

To understand that the church is here for mission has practical implications. "Imagine," writes Bevans, "what the structure of the church would be like if we recognized that it is mission that needs to be first, and not the church. Ministry would exist for the mission and not for itself. So many things that bog us down today would simply fall away: clerical privilege, restrictions on lay people's ministry, the role of women in the ministry and decision making in the church. What would be important is not people's roles in the *church*, but how ministers might equip people for ministry in the world."

There is a dizzying array of images for the church. But the chosen part is clear: It is *us*. And we are here for *God*.

The church is a spiritual community that participates in the saving, healing, and forgiving work of Jesus Christ whom God has sent. The church is you and me and everyone else being Christ to our brothers and sisters in Christ, on the spot where we're standing, and in all places and at all times.

We are the place where Jesus and the Father dwell. That is our purpose: to be what we already are.

And that is why I stay in the church. It is where I am.

16

A Mass of Energy

It is no longer I who live, but it is Christ who lives in me.
—Galatians 2:20, NRSV

Going to Mass does not mean that we shall be filled with
warm feelings for other members of the congregation.
Probably not! But it does imply a gradual transformation of
who I am—"I and no longer I"—discovering God and myself
in the stranger, and God in the core of my being. . . .
The slow working of grace will free me to be sent at
the end. Why go to church? To be sent from it.
—Timothy Radcliffe, OP, Why Go to Church?

The church was dark. It was six-thirty on a winter morning and there wasn't enough sun to brighten the stained-
glass window in front of the altar. I was serving Mass for
an old priest who faced a marble cross hanging beneath
the window. He leaned over a round piece of bread as thin
as a holy card and whispered, "Hoc . . . est . . . enim . . .
corpus . . . meum!" I jangled bells welded together like
a three-leaf clover three times. Father genuflected and

raised the body of Christ high in the air. Behind us a handful of women and men bowed their heads and tapped their breasts three times. Another morning. Another Mass. Another miracle to start the day.

I rarely missed daily Mass until I was twenty-eight years old. I went from being an altar boy to being a teenage seminarian. Then from ages twenty-five to twenty-eight I presided at Mass as a priest. I left the priesthood when I was twenty-eight to marry. Vickie and I went to Mass every week, and I sometimes went to a noon mass on my lunch hour in the city. We were active in our parish, took our boys to Mass every Sunday, and taught them the faith. The boys never much liked church, and as they grew up stopped going to Mass. That bothered Vickie. Not me. They were, as we both knew, wonderful, kind young men with strong values. I understood. I was finding it a chore to go to church myself. The sermons were dreadful. Hardly anyone in the pews said the prayers or sang the hymns, including me. None of this was anything new, but for the first time I started to skip Sundays. Today Vickie still goes every week, and I attend irregularly. Only four out of ten Catholics, according to a 2008 study by the Center for Applied Research in the Apostolate (CARA) attend Mass regularly. For the first time in American religious history, more Protestants go to church on Sunday than Catholics. Most Catholics do not believe that missing Mass is a sin. Other surveys show that only a third of Catholics believe that the bread and wine become the body and blood of Christ, while two-thirds say they are just symbolic reminders of Jesus.

Writing this chapter brings me up short. The Eucharist is at the heart of Catholicism, and I'm not that interested anymore. What have I forgotten? What do I need to know? What can I write that is true, honest, and helpful? What is the chosen part of the Mass, the spiritual part that is so clear that I cannot escape its light?

The Mass is a drama in three acts (offertory, consecration, and communion), but it is not a theater piece. If we are looking for entertainment, we're better off going to the movies. The Eucharist is a spiritual happening but not a magic trick. If we're looking for magic, we watch David Copperfield. The Mass seems to take forever but is even longer: "God's gifts are given through the slow transformation of who we are," writes Fr. Radcliffe, "God's undramatic, noiseless work, recreating us as people who have faith, hope, and charity." The energy of the Eucharist is not automatic. We know too many people who have received communion for decades and are still miserable. The invitation to Eucharistic grace comes with an RSVP. The energy of Mass is equal to our willingness to empty our egos.

Just what is this mystery called Eucharist?

> This teaching is difficult; who can accept it?
> —JOHN 6:60
>
> The Eucharist is a mystery not because it is mysterious, but because it is a sign of God's secret purpose, which is to unite all things in Christ.
> —TIMOTHY RADCLIFFE, *WHY GO TO CHURCH?*

The Eucharist is a sacrament, a symbol, a reality, a sacrifice, a reminder, a remembrance, a meal, a thanksgiving, an invitation, and a gift.

Let's break it down.

As a sacrament, Eucharist is at once symbol and reality. The Catholic novelist Flannery O'Connor famously said, "If it's [just] a symbol, to hell with it." No symbol is just a symbol. A symbol is a thing we can see, hear, taste, or touch that represents a reality that is invisible and intangible yet equally present. Every word we speak is a symbol. When we promise "to love and to cherish" in marriage, the words point to a commitment and covenant beyond words. Words are powerful. They are powerful because they stand for something even more powerful and no less real. Eucharist stands for— and really is—the presence of Christ in our lives.

The Eucharist reminds us that Jesus Christ, the Son of God, came into the world to show us that we, too, are born of God, to teach us to love ourselves and to love everyone as he loved us, as brothers and sisters in Christ. It is a remembrance that Jesus made a singular sacrifice to stop all scapegoating once and for all, to end all sacrifice of innocent victims to an angry God and instead to know him as Abba *(Daddy)* and accept his gift of love as did the prodigal son, who had forgotten, and then re-membered, who he was and that he could never really leave home. The Eucharist is a remembrance of our salvation that takes place now and always and—how wonderful!— cannot be reversed.

The Eucharist is a spiritual meal. It is not an actual meal any more than the sacrament of baptism is a bath. It isn't chewing on Jesus' flesh but on his teachings. It isn't drinking his corpuscles but his life. We get hung up on the doctrine of transubstantiation by asking *how*. It took the Council of Trent six years (1545–1551) to define that word, and scholars are still debating the details. All we need to know is *what*. "I am the bread of life. Whoever comes to me will never be hungry, and whoever believes in me will never be thirsty" (John 6:35, NRSV). In Eucharist we partake of the Wisdom of God. Fr. Radcliffe writes in *Why Go to Church?*:

> So when we eat the body of Jesus and drink his blood, it is not as if we were to roast our local bishop and devour him at a parish picnic. We are accepting the gift of the one who is Wisdom Incarnate. God's Wisdom is not just a divine intelligence. Wisdom was with God when the world was created, and made it to be our home.

In Eucharist we give thanks for the gift of knowing we have never left Eden, never left home. Jesus comes to assure us that Abba is still with us. Eucharist is an invitation to consume the truth of our being. To be one with Jesus and everyone everywhere who is, in truth, also within us as we are in them and all of us are in the Father. Perhaps the most important words of the Mass are the very last spoken:

"The Mass is ended, go in peace to love and serve the Lord."
"Thanks be to God!"

The Latin words are, literally, "Go, this is your mission!" Our mission is to go out and be like Jesus who has come to us again. The Eucharist is not just a symbol and not just about Sunday; it's about the presence of Christ on Monday and about remembering who we are in the mystical body of Christ.

I'm still Catholic because I keep forgetting what's really important and need reminders. The Eucharist is a reminder and a remembering, an invitation and a gift. I'm pretty sure I'll go to church more frequently than when I did before writing this chapter. Thanks be to God.

17

A Garden of Spiritual Paths

There is not, and never has been, a single Christian
spirituality, nor a single Catholic spirituality.
—RICHARD P. MCBRIEN, *CATHOLICISM*

It was just a local cable show, but the other guest called
me a "supermarket Catholic," and I got emotional. "So
what's so bad about that?" I said. "The Catholic Church
is the greatest spiritual supermarket the world has ever
known! It has aisles that never end and its spiritual fruits
are enough to nourish you for eternity—not to mention
the meats, potatoes, and vegetables! No one can eat everything at once. The problem is that the church is promoting only a small portion of what's available in its spiritual
storehouse, and a lot of people are hungry for what's been
hidden, including the infinite variety of desserts!"

That'll teach him.

The term "supermarket Catholic" soon devolved into
"cafeteria Catholic," another derogatory term used to
divide allegedly picky Catholics from those who simply eat
what is put on their plates. But I stand by my outburst. The

Catholic Church is not only a spiritual supermarket but is a garden of spiritual paths that go in unexpected directions but always lead back to the fountain of life at its center. Fruit trees line every path and the oranges and pears and peaches are always in reach. When it comes to spirituality, the Catholic Church is a Garden of Eden!

Yes, I get carried away.

If God can work through me, he can work through anyone.
—FRANCIS OF ASSISI

If [a man] wishes to be sure of the road he travels on, he must close his eyes and walk in the dark.
—JOHN OF THE CROSS, *DARK NIGHT OF THE SOUL*

Run, jump, shout and do whatever you like as long as you don't sin.
—DON BOSCO

The garden was planted through the centuries by spiritual masters such as St. Francis, St. Benedict, and many others who founded various religious communities. And for centuries discerning Catholics have followed their paths, each one different, each one packed with the same rich soil. They have experienced the earthy joy of the Franciscans, the simplicity of the Cistercians, the compassion of the Little Sisters of the Poor. Some choose to stay on the straight and narrow with the rule of the Benedictines; others elect to circle the globe with Maryknoll missioners. Many like to taste the sweet mysticism of the Carmelites, while others bite into the preaching of the Dominicans. Catholics build themselves up with the spiritual exercises of the Jesuits, and enjoy small pleasures with the playful Salesians. The simple appeal of these founders speaks through the centuries.

Let nothing disturb you,
Let nothing frighten you,
All things are passing away,
God does not change.
Patience obtains all things
Whoever has God lacks nothing;
God alone is enough.

—TERESA OF ÁVILA

Each religious order has a unique way of seeing life from a spiritual perspective that is just right for someone. And the good thing is, you don't have to give up everything, leave home, and become a sister, brother, or priest to adapt their path in your own life.

The number of women and men who live in consecrated religious communities is decreasing as their age increases, but the number of laypeople who are expressing the same spiritual charism in their lives is multiplying like loaves and fishes. Catholics are doing their homework and are not only familiar with the garden of spiritual paths but find themselves attracted to one or more of them. They get up and feed their kids and go to work and eat out with their friends and, at the same time, endeavor to express a spirituality that is proven and appealing.

Some actually attach themselves to a particular religious order or society without ever leaving home. Franciscans, Carmelites, and Dominicans call them "seculars." The Jesuits and Maryknoll Fathers and Brothers call them "affiliates." The Benedictines call them "oblates." They live in cities or suburbs or rural areas far away from the abbey or monastery or motherhouse but walk the spiritual path in their daily lives.

Catharine Henningsen, an accomplished journalist, has been an associate of the Sisters of the Sacred Heart for most of her adult life. As I write this, she is taking care of Sister Margaret Hayes, a Sacred Heart sister and former psychiatrist in her early eighties, at her home in Connecticut. Catherine doesn't do this as part of her role as an associate but because she has a habit of being loving. This is what it means to Catharine to be an associate of the Sacred Heart:

> The charism of the Society—"to show forth the love of the heart of Christ"—has always been highly attractive to me. Now, with Margaret here, I find myself learning more each day about what it means to live it. Margaret's physical hardships now may be great, but it never stops her from getting the loving part right.
>
> Our foundress, St. Madeleine Sophie Barat, is credited with saying, "for a single child I would have founded the Society." I like to think of the "single child" in each person I meet and to ask myself would I give all-in-all for that one person? What I come to, thinking that way, is another of the Society's great spiritual lessons: the practice of being fully present to each one. There are so many paths to finding Christ in the other, but Sophie's is the voice I hear.

Ronnie Gilligan is a Maryknoll affiliate from Long Island who leaves home for three months each year to help missioners. She's been to Thailand, Nepal, Cambodia, Bolivia, Albania, and recently St. Stephen's Mission Church at the Wind River Indian Reservation in Wyoming, where she taught religious education, brought communion to the sick, and "shoveled snow and horse manure." Ronnie writes in *Maryknoll* magazine:

> My association with Maryknoll has helped put words to my beliefs that we don't have to teach God because God is already there. Our job is to help people recognize God in themselves. One night with the family I was preparing for First Communion, the topic came up about what Jesus looked like. Thinking about where the historical Jesus lived and that he and his family were frequently in the sun in the deserts, with no mention of peeling skin or freckles, we concluded that Jesus probably looked more like my Native American hosts than like me.
>
> By night's end we were talking about prayer and where we find God. "God lives in me and I'm Indian," said one of the children. I will remember that for a long, long time.

Few of us have the kind of commitment that Catharine and Ronnie do. But not only do we not have to become a religious to follow a traditional spiritual path, we don't even have to become an associate or an affiliate. We can follow an established path all on our own. That's what a large number of Catholics do. John Michael Talbot, founder of the Brothers and Sisters of Charity, writes in his book *The World Is My Cloister*:

> For every person who joins up as an oblate, secular, domestic or associate, there are hundreds, perhaps even thousands more who find inspiration from simply reflecting on the monastic saints and movements. This is a totally indefinable and innumerable group of folks just trying to make it through the day without totally losing their spiritual footing or perhaps just now finding it. They are Catholics and non-Catholics, Christians and non-Christians, believers and unbelievers. In a way this new phenomenon is a new Pentecost, an event of the Holy Spirit firing people's desire for God.

So just as you don't have to be Catholic to manifest the reign of God, you don't have to be Catholic to walk in the garden of spiritual paths. I like to play on all of them. A lot of us are still Catholic simply because we need the exercise. It's even better than a supermarket.

18

Fruits of the Spirit

Truth is what works.
—William James

The proof of the pudding is the eating.
—Don Quixote

But the fruit of the Spirit is love, joy, peace, patience,
kindness, generosity, faithfulness, gentleness, and
self-control. There is no law against such things.
—Galatians 5:22, NRSV

The Christian ideal has not been tried and found wanting.
It has been found difficult and left untried.
—G. K. Chesterton, What's Wrong with the World

Well, you've just read the whole chapter. You can move on now.

Still here? Okay, here is how it breaks down.

If a tree on the spiritual path bears good fruit, it's a good tree. The fruits that fall on a valid spiritual path are love, joy, peace, patience, kindness, goodness, faithfulness, gentleness, and discipline. If you experience these spiritual qualities, you are on the right spiritual path for you and can do no wrong. If you experience fear, anger, and joylessness, it's time to consider a road not taken. But before you do, it's wise to ask yourself, *Have I given the trail I'm on a fair trial? Did I study the map at the beginning and along the way?* Most folks stray from the church because other Catholics have given them a bogus map or led them astray by their example. Who can blame them for taking a road trip? All this book suggests is that it wouldn't hurt to "give peace a chance"—the "peace that is beyond all understanding" (Philippians 4:7)—before laying cement over the paths of spirituality Catholicism has to offer. If those fruits of love, joy, and peace still don't manifest, then it's time to go exploring.

At times like this it's beneficial to look at other spiritual paths without abandoning our own. When we study other traditions, we often find our own spirituality enhanced. But that happens only when we're as interested in rediscovering the chosen part of our own religion as we are the chosen part in another. We embrace the baby before we throw out the bathwater. We don't give up the ship even if we're hanging on to the bark of Peter with our fingernails. Maybe a new wind will come along and blow us in a better direction. The breezy immediacy of Eastern spirituality has enriched my appreciation of Catholicism, and Catholic spirituality has led me to appreciate Eastern wisdom. My friend Jack Shea likes to joke about our seminary days, "While everybody else was reading Aquinas, Mike was studying Zen." I read

Aquinas, all three volumes. I just thought Basho was a better poet. Many Catholics today who are frustrated with the church choose to study Buddhism and Zen Masters much more than they do the spiritual teachings of Jesus and the saints. It doesn't make sense to turn our back on fruits that nourish us. When we sincerely look at both trees, we see lovely parallels:

✛ "Your everyday mind—that is the way." Wu-men
✛ "God is found among the pots and pans." St. Thérèse of Lisieux
✛ "Let the children come to me for theirs is the kingdom of heaven." Jesus (Matthew 19:14)
✛ "Children get to heaven by playing." Zen saying
✛ "Overcome anger with love, overcome evil with good, overcome the miser by giving, overcome the liar with truth." Buddha
✛ "Love your enemies, do good to those who hate you, bless those who curse you, pray for those who abuse you. From anyone who takes away your coat do not withhold even your shirt. Give to everyone who begs from you; and if anyone takes away your goods, do not ask for them again." Jesus (Luke 6:27–31)
✛ "The thief left it behind / the moon / at my window!" Ryokan
✛ "If we could see the miracle of a single flower clearly, our whole life would change." Buddha
✛ "Look at the lilies of the field!" Jesus (Matthew 6:28)
✛ "Every moment comes to us pregnant with a command from God, only to pass on and plunge into eternity, there

to remain forever what we have made of it." St. Francis de Sales

✛ "If you walk, just walk. / If you sit, just sit. / But whatever you do, don't wobble." Unmon

✛ "If you do not tend for one another, then who is there to tend for you? If you wish to tend for me, tend the sick. Consider others as yourself." Buddha

✛ "I tell you the truth, whatever you did for one of the least of these brothers of mine, you did for me. . . . Do unto others as you would have them do unto you." Jesus (Matthew 25:40 and Matthew 7:12)

Now, to paraphrase my friend John Lennon, who got in trouble for saying the Beatles were more popular than Jesus and then had to apologize; I'm not saying that Buddhism is more popular than Catholicism or Catholicism is better or both are equal. I'm only saying there are lovely expressions of truth everywhere, and if one bears good fruit for you, it is valid. If it doesn't, hey, that's okay too. "Road trip!"

Can we know for sure that we are on the right spiritual path? Is it enough to believe that God said it was the right path? That works for many people. But since you're reading this book—and I hope you've rediscovered a lot of treasures stored in the attic of Catholic consciousness so far—that may not be working all that well for you. After all, belief implies doubt, just as doubt depends on belief. We can't say "I believe" without confirming the possibility of doubt. How can we *know* a spiritual path is valid for us?

Jesus put it very simply, he said: "By their fruits you shall know them" (Matthew 7:20). Further, he said, "When you know the truth, it will make you free" (John 8:32).

We *can* know whether or not an idea is spiritually valid in our lives. We don't have to take somebody else's word for it. We don't have to read a Gallup poll or watch Dr. Phil or leave our experiences at the door of the church. We don't have to agree or disagree with anyone. We have only to consider if there is more love, joy, peace, patience, kindness, goodness, faithfulness, gentleness, and discipline in our lives than there was before. Now that may or may not happen right away, and nobody is going to be spiritually awake and aware all the time. But it will happen if we are sincere in our spiritual search.

Ralph Waldo Emerson said, "Life is a journey, not a destination." So did Aerosmith. It must be true. Jesus was stronger: "I am the Way, the Truth, and the Life" (John 14:6). The way is a journey among trees that bear good fruit. The tree is valid not because it is true; it is true because it bears good fruit. How many of us have taken the time to understand what Jesus meant when he said those words? Before we leave something, it's a good idea to understand, on our own, what it is we are leaving.

I'm still Catholic because Catholicism as I've grown to understand it over the years brings me love, joy, peace, patience, kindness, goodness, faithfulness, gentleness, and discipline. I stay in the church even as it drives me nuts, like my family of birth, because it's been a good home for me and I can always take road trips and come back revived, and be grateful for the spiritual garden I never really left, with its abundant fruits that always stay fresh.

19

The Seamless Garment of Life

When the soldiers crucified Jesus, they took his clothes,
dividing them into four shares, one for each of them,
with Jesus' cloak remaining. This garment was seamless,
woven in one piece from top to bottom.
—JOHN 19:23

When Chicago's Cardinal Bernardin was dying of cancer, Chicagoans responded as they did when they heard that President Roosevelt had died. The announcement brought the city of broad shoulders to its knees. The *Tribune* quoted the Cardinal as saying he faced death with peace and that it was a gift from God.

Jeremy Langford, a young editor from Loyola Press, was working with the cardinal on a memoir that after Bernardin's death would become the inspirational bestseller *The Gift of Peace.* Jeremy asked the cardinal, "Did I misunderstand what you said to the press? Was the gift from God knowing when you are going to die or the sense of peace?" The Cardinal smiled and answered, "Many people misunderstood. It's interesting, isn't it? We can understand cancer but peace is less comprehensible."

After his death not only Chicagoans but Catholics everywhere would remember Joseph Bernardin for teaching us how to die with dignity. Few would remember how he taught a whole world to live with dignity through his profoundly Catholic idea, the Seamless Garment of Life. Isn't it interesting? We can understand the inevitability of death, but the sanctity of life is less comprehensible.

Here is Cardinal Bernardin's gift to the world.

It is not a belief but a *knowing* that all of us are one. The Seamless Garment of Life is not a theory but a principle that all life is sacred, from womb to tomb, in the unborn and the dying, in the murderer on death row and the mother in a coma, in the soldier in Afghanistan and the homeless family in Iraq, in the child abused by a pedophile and the pensioner who can't afford a doctor, in the oil-poisoned Gulf and the coal mines of Pennsylvania, in the Arab and in the Israeli. "When human life is considered 'cheap' or easily expendable in one area," said Cardinal Bernardin, "eventually nothing is held as sacred and all lives are in jeopardy."

Sister Eileen Egan (1911–2000), a cofounder of the peace organization Pax Christi, coined the phrase *Seamless Garment of Life* in 1973. A decade later Bernardin (1928–1996) turned the metaphor into a consistent ethic of life. It became a cloak of moral issues woven together as seamlessly as Jesus' tunic and was an endeavor to bring unity to Catholic teaching. He wrote:

If one contends, as we do, that the right of every fetus to be born should be protected by civil law and supported by civil consensus, then our moral, political and economic responsibilities do not stop at the moment of birth. Those who defend the right to life of the weakest among us must be equally visible in support of the quality of life of the powerless among us: the old and the young, the hungry and the homeless, the undocumented immigrant and the unemployed worker. Such a quality of life posture translates into specific political and economic positions on tax policy, employment generation, welfare policy, nutrition and feeding programs, and health care. Consistency means we cannot have it both ways. We cannot urge a compassionate society and vigorous public policy to protect the rights of the unborn and then argue that compassion and significant public programs on behalf of the needy undermine the moral fiber of society or are beyond the proper scope of government responsibility. Right to life and quality of life complement each other in domestic society.

While this was bold and Catholic to the core, the cardinal positioned the teaching in such a way that it was not only religious but also universal so everyone could come closer to an ethic on the sanctity of life. But politicians soon used the principle for their own agendas. Democrats used it to argue against unjust war, capital punishment, and economic oppression, while Republicans co-opted the principle to reinforce their opposition to abortion, euthanasia, and stem-cell research. Few moved toward the center. They could understand their preconceptions, but consistency was less comprehensible, just as would be Bernardin's gift of peace.

The cardinal knew this was a hard teaching. His desire was to sew the sanctity of life with the quality of life, to defend life and to promote it. He understood the differences but also saw the connections and wanted to build a bridge between pro-life conservatives and social justice liberals. Slowly the idea took root in Catholic consciousness. In 1994 the U.S. Conference of Catholic Bishops endorsed the principle as an alternative to violence. In 1995 Pope John Paul II issued the encyclical *The Gospel of Life*, encouraging "a culture of life" over a "culture of death." He wrote:

> Where life is involved, the service of charity must be profoundly consistent. It cannot tolerate bias and discrimination, for human life is sacred and inviolable at every stage and in every situation: it is an indivisible good. We need then to "show care" for all life and for the life of everyone.

Cardinal Bernardin died in peace in 1996.

The Catholic Church has always based its moral beliefs on the dignity of the human person. The unique contribution of Cardinal Bernardin was to weave the disparate threads into a whole cloth. The result has been increased clarity in church teachings about modern warfare, abortion, capital punishment, genetics, and care for the terminally ill. It is still not an easy teaching, but for the first time in a long time there are fewer "single issue" Catholics and more who think twice—and three times— about contemporary moral dilemmas. Thanks to more comprehensive education on life-and-death issues, most people are no longer on the far left or far right of these matters but are sitting squarely on the middle of the fence, an uncomfortable but honest place to be. More and more, people are seeing the unity of life and their responsibility not to rip it apart as the soldiers did Christ's garments, but to keep it whole.

I'm still Catholic because the church has a consistent ethic of life. The seamless garment is not always comfortable, but it fits all sizes.

20

The Church's Best-Kept Secret

I beg you, look for the words "social justice" or "economic justice" on your church website. If you find it, run as fast as you can. Social justice and economic justice, they are code words. Now, am I advising people to leave their church? Yes!
—GLENN BECK, MARCH 2, 2010

Now the whole group of those who believed were of one heart and soul, and no one claimed private ownership of any possessions, but everything they owned was held in common. . . . There was not a needy person among them, for as many as owned lands or houses sold them and brought the proceeds of what was sold. They laid it at the apostles' feet, and it was distributed to each as any had need.
—ACTS OF THE APOSTLES 4:32–35, CIRCA 112

The difference between communism and Christianity? Communism says you must be good. Christianity says it's good to be good.

Catholic social thought is not political but spiritual. It springs from the knowledge that each of us is made in the image and likeness of God. Just as a sunbeam cannot be separated from the sun or any other sunbeam, none of us can be separated from God or any other human being. We are all radiances of one light.

Catholic social teaching is founded on the principle of solidarity: a spiritual awareness that each of us is responsible for the good of all of us. It is knowing that when a family in Chicago gets food stamps, a city is richer; when a family in Maine receives health care, a state is healthier; when taxes from a corporation in Manhattan help provide shelter for a homeless family on the Gulf Coast, a country is stronger; and when a wealthy country sends AIDS medicine to families in Nigeria, the entire world is blessed.

Catholic social thought traces back to the Old Testament, but its official teachings date back to the time of Oliver Twist, who got into trouble for asking, "Please, sir, may I have some more?" That was the best of times and the worst of times, a time of liberating wealth and suffocating poverty, a time of robber barons and child laborers. In 1891 Pope Leo XIII wrote his historic encyclical *Rerum Novarum (The Condition of Labor)*, which addressed social and economic injustice:

> Let it be taken for granted that workman and employer should, as a rule, make free agreements, and in particular should agree freely as to wages; nevertheless, there is a dictate of natural justice more imperious and

ancient than any bargain between man and man, that remuneration should be sufficient to maintain the wage-earner in reasonable and frugal comfort. If through necessity or fear of a worse evil the work-man accept harder conditions because an employer or contractor will afford him no better, he is made the victim of force and injustice.

The encyclical also criticizes the socialism of Karl Marx and defends the right to own private property. Mr. Beck would applaud it.

What has always disturbed critics is that the encyclical, and all the teachings of the church on these issues, put responsibility not only on individuals but also on institutions—economic, political, and social. The church teaches that human beings have a fundamental right to life, food, shelter, health care, education, and employment, and that government has a moral responsibility to support these rights. The Catholic principle of subsidiarity holds that when basic needs are not being met at the grassroots level, then it is not only necessary but imperative that government, first local, then state and federal, do what it can to help. The church doesn't tell the state what its public policies or technical solutions should be; it simply does what it is meant to do: offer moral challenges that flow from its spiritual vision: "When I was hungry you gave me something to eat, when I was thirsty you gave me something to drink, when I was a stranger you invited me in, when I needed clothes you clothed me, when I was sick you looked after me, and when I was in prison you came to visit me. I tell you the truth: whatever you do for the least of these my brethren you do for me" (Matthew 25:30–41, NIV).

> As followers of Christ, we are challenged to make a fundamental "option for the poor"–to speak for the voiceless, to defend the defenseless, to assess life styles, policies, and social institutions in terms of their impact on the poor. This "option for the poor" does not mean pitting one group against another, but rather, strengthening the whole community by assisting those who are the most vulnerable. As Christians, we are called to respond to the needs of all our brothers and sisters, but those with the greatest needs require the greatest response.
>
> —ECONOMIC JUSTICE FOR ALL: PASTORAL LETTER ON CATHOLIC SOCIAL TEACHING AND THE U.S. ECONOMY, U.S. BISHOPS, 1986

Since *Rerum Novarum* in 1891, the Catholic Church has issued numerous documents and statements on social and economic justice. The issues have expanded to include religious freedom, the environment, immigration, modern warfare, and torture. Running throughout everything is a primary concern for the poor and vulnerable.

The church in its teachings endeavors to have, or put on, the mind of Christ (1 Corinthians 2:16). Jesus was born in a stable. His parents were refugees. He lived among the poor, fed multitudes with the only food available, was friendly with the rich and the marginal and brought them together, and when he died his only possession was a seamless garment. The only valid criticism of the church is not that its social teachings go too far but that it doesn't always practice what it teaches.

The chosen part is clear. Mother Teresa expressed it by her life and in her simple words: "Whoever the poorest of the poor are, they are Christ for us—Christ under the guise of human suffering." If you see the words "social justice" or "economic justice" on a sign in front of your church, you can know it is pointing in the right direction.

Catholic Social Teaching, according to the Orbis book of the same name, is "our best-kept secret." It's a secret because nobody wants to hear about it. I'm still Catholic because it challenges me to be a better Christian.

21

Everyone Has a Guardian Angel

Look, Daddy. Teacher says, every time a bell rings
an angel gets his wings!
—Zuzu Bailey, *It's a Wonderful Life*

I believe in angels.
—ABBA, "I Have a Dream"

In a 2007 Gallup poll, three out of four Americans said, "I believe in angels." Americans trust angels ten times more than they do their congressmen. That makes sense.

Angels are a traditional Catholic idea, but how well do we understand what we believe in? How many of us think of angels as heavenly Tinkerbells? It never hurts to be like Zuzu Bailey and, when we take our favorite ornament out of the box, polish it and hold it in front of our eyes before placing it on the tree. We may see something new. Does an angel really get its wings every time a Christmas bell rings?

Of course it does!

Now on to the next question. What is an angel? An angel is a messenger from God.

Like the UPS man?

No, an angel is more like the postman. But unlike a postman in Alabama, say, who delivers a letter from Alaska to a third person in Mobile, the angelic messenger and its message are *one*. An angel is a good idea from God.

The message comes from God to a child of God, just like that. That's why we can't see angels. They're instant.

"An angel gives us a closer idea of God," writes Meister Eckhart. "That is all an angel is: an idea of God."

The bible story of Abraham and Isaac suggests how it works, and maybe doesn't work. Abraham was the father of the Israelites and had a beloved son named Isaac who was his heir. Abraham thought he heard an angel of God telling him to sacrifice Isaac. In those days people believed they would please God by killing people for God because God was still angry with Adam and Eve. So Abraham took his son to a far place, bound him on an altar, put a knife to his throat, and then heard a stronger message: "Abraham! Abraham! Do not lay a hand on the boy. Do not do anything to him!" That voice was the real angel.

Then Abraham heard the first voice again: "Now I know that you fear God because you have not withheld from me your son, your only son." That may have been the voice of human guilt getting in the last word. So Abraham went and sacrificed a ram.

That was the most momentous turning point in religious history since Adam's son Cain killed his brother, Abel. It marked the beginning of the end to human sacrifice.

Centuries later the same angel assured the psalmist that God does not delight in sacrifice or is pleased with burnt offerings (Psalm 51:16). And centuries after that the Son of God would willingly lay down his life for all of us and rise from the dead to prove that everything he taught was true. Before his death Jesus said: "If you had known what this means, 'I desire mercy and not sacrifice,' you would not have condemned the guiltless" (Matthew 12:7).

Jesus' death was the most momentous turning point in all history. It was a lesson so profound that no one could look at sacrificial scapegoating of an innocent victim in the same way ever again.

We know today that God does not want us to sacrifice our children. Or anybody else's children. Or even a ram. God desires only good. And he tells us through angels.

But we don't always hear them. The alarming voices of human history drown out "the still, small voice" (1 Kings 19:12, KJV). Some of us still haven't heard the angel's message to Abraham or learned the lesson of Jesus' sacrifice, and we commit "little murders" all our lives. Sometimes we hear mixed messages, as it appears Abraham did, and become "double-minded, and unstable in every way" (James 1:8, NRSV). We need to discern the good ideas from God beneath the static of fear, anger, and guilt. We know the message is an angel only when it has the qualities of the Sender, not of mere human nature. If the idea brings love and peace, as the second did to Abraham, we know it has found the right address. St. Ignatius of Loyola teaches us how to recognize God's messages: "the action of the good angel is delicate, gentle, delightful. It may be compared to a drop of water penetrating a sponge. The action of the evil spirit upon such souls is violent, noisy, and disturbing. It may be compared to a drop of water falling upon a stone." (*The Spiritual Exercises of St. Ignatius*, #335, Puhl trans.)

Catholicism says we are surrounded by angels—God's blessed ideas for us—just as surely as if we were in the center of a fresco painted by Raphael. Angels guided Mary and Joseph on their flight from Bethlehem to Egypt. Angels guarded Jesus in the desert and comforted him in the Garden of Gethsemane. Jesus counseled all of us: "See that you never look down upon one of these children, for I say to you that their angels in heaven always see the face of my Father who is in heaven" (Matthew 18:10, adapted). Was he not telling us that children see the face of God more clearly than adults because they are open to visits from angels? "Angels," writes Richard McBrien in *Catholicism*, "are reminders that there is more to the created order than what we actually see, feel, hear, and taste."

To be open to angels is to be open to miracles. A miracle is an angel heard.

I'm still Catholic because I learned in Catholic school that I have a guardian angel. That was a small but significant turning point in my history. You know, I haven't said the following prayer in a long, long time, but I think I will now. It is the first prayer I ever learned.

Angel of God, my guardian dear
to whom God's love commits me here.
Ever this day be at my side
to light and guard, to rule and guide.
Amen.

22

Benedicamus Domino!
Or, Catholics Like to Party

Wherever the Catholic sun doth shine,
There's always laughter and good red wine.
At least I've always found it so.
Benedicamus Domino!
—Hilaire Belloc

Have you ever been to an Irish wake? An Italian wedding? Polka night at St. Stanislaus Kostka parish in Chicago? Oktoberfest in Milwaukee? Have you ever sung and swayed with the gospel choir at Holy Name of Jesus Church in Los Angeles? Taken your kids to the Carnival of Fun at St. Catherine of Sienna in Riverside, Connecticut? Celebrated being alive during the three-week fiesta in San Antonio? If you're frustrated with the Catholic Church, maybe you need to get around more.

Catholicism is an ethnic religion, a coat of many colors, a kaleidoscope in which dazzling pieces of colored glass keep turning to the light and meeting at the center. It's a religion of pipe organs and concertinas, kettle drums and bongos, triangles and trombones. You can smell freshly baked bread or sizzling sausage or good old American hamburgers at any old Catholic picnic or bake sale or feast in any old Catholic parish on any old summer night of the year. Catholics like to get together and eat cholesterol and drink beer and have fun with friends. It's a Jesus thing.

Jesus palled around with people who liked to have fun. His first miracle was turning water into wine at a wedding party. The people who didn't like him called him a glutton and a drunkard because he associated with sinners (Matthew 11:18). Do you think the Last Supper was a somber affair? It was a going-away party at which Jesus gave the whole world an everlasting gift. And when he rose from the dead and met two of his friends who didn't recognize him, he said, "Let's eat." They recognized him in the breaking of the bread. Can you imagine how heartily Jesus must have laughed?

The saints liked to party too. St. Brigid, God bless her Irish soul, said: "I would like a great lake of beer for the King of kings. I would like to be watching heaven's family drinking it through all eternity." St. Teresa of Ávila prayed, "From silly devotions and sour-faced saints, good Lord, deliver us!" The greatest Catholic host may have been Angelo Roncalli (1881–1963), aka Pope John XXIII, who threw a party for the whole church called Vatican II. He opened the windows and beautiful doves flew in and angels flew out from the hidden deposit of faith. It was a party of ideas, a celebration of the chosen part of things. Here was a man who knew what was real. Jean Maalouf in his book *Pope John XXIII: Essential Writings* tells this story:

> A few days after his coronation John held a special audience for his family, a privilege granted to each new occupant of St. Peter's Chair. The Roncallis entered the apartments in the apostolic palace timidly. The splendor of the place troubled their simple souls. Finally, bashful and confused, they stood before the white-clad figure of the pope. In their confusion they dropped their little presents. Peasant bread, ham, and wine, packed in brightly colored handkerchiefs, all tumbled to the floor. John looked at their staring eyes and open mouths. Although the comedy of the situation did not escape him, he spoke reassuringly: "Don't be afraid. It's only me."

That's pretty much what Jesus said after his death when he suddenly appeared to the disciples trembling in the upper room (John 20:19). Jesus loved his friends, had good times with them, and taught them not only how to die but how to live.

If Catholics have always liked to party, the best is yet to come. Joy is infusing the Catholic Church in the

> I am about to create new heavens and a new earth.
> —Isaiah 65:17, NRSV

United States with the emergence of Hispanic Catholics from Mexico, Puerto Rico, Central and South America.

Hispanics/Latinos(as) have contributed 71 percent of the growth of the Church since 1960. More than half the Catholics in the United States under age twenty-five are of Hispanic descent, as are 25 percent of all laypeople engaged in diocesan ministry programs. It's time to take out our most colorful clothes and get ready to salivate at the next church picnic where Italian sausage, American hamburgers, and German lager will be joined by tacos, enchiladas, and burritos. Hispanic Americans, just like the immigrants of the early twentieth century, are bringing something new and rich to the church of the early twenty-first century—and it's not just great food.

A few years ago, Fr. Virgil Elizondo, who is both a pastor in San Antonio and a professor at Notre Dame, asked his American quilt of friends, "When are you the happiest?" The responses revealed an interesting difference between U.S.A. Americans and Mexican Americans. He writes in his book-in-progress, *Why Mexico Matters*:

> For the most part, U.S.A. Americans responded with an "I" answer such as when I am doing good for others, when I have achieved my goal, when I have paid all my credit cards, when I go fishing, golfing, or skiing, when I am home after work drinking a beer and watching a good ball game, when I get a good bonus and so on. With the Mexican Americans the responses were generally in the "We" such as during a family celebration, when we are playing a good soccer game, enjoying a good meal with friends, at home with the family when the kids are not crying and

hollering. In short it seems that for U.S.A. Americans happiness exists in the individual while for the Mexican it exists in the togetherness. One emphasizes the individual while the other emphasizes the relationship.

This is one of the chosen parts of things. Community. Togetherness. Oneness. Just what the party needs.

I'm going to stick around in the church because a new *abrazo* is coming. I wish I could stick around to the beginning of the twenty-second century. Who knows what *la familia* will look like then? One thing is certain. It will throw a party.

23

God Is Found among the Pots and Pans

Work is love made visible.
—Khalil Gibran

God lives also among the pots and pans.
—St. Teresa of Ávila

Artie and I were now in our forties. We had both left the priesthood to marry years ago. Artie was the funniest guy I'd ever known, but here we were drinking beer and sharing memories and he was sad. "You're so lucky," he said. "You have a good job. You edit books with big ideas. You hang around with brains. You even know Edward Schillebeeckx, for crissakes! And here I am, selling toilet paper to Greek restaurants. . . ."

"Artie," I said, "at least people *use* your paper. My books just sit there."

We ordered a pitcher.

Artie didn't know that I was frustrated too. "I don't make enough money either, Art, and people drive me crazy sometimes too. I once asked my publicity director who her favorite author was. She said, 'Albert Camus.' I said, 'But he's dead.' She said, 'Exactly.'"

"The only thing I know how to do well," Artie said, "is to be a priest." Truth was, Artie could do everything well. But his happiest work moments were as a priest. He was one of the best.

Is there such a thing as finding joy in our job no matter what it is? Is one kind of work inherently more fulfilling than another? Or is it our job to bring joy to whatever we do?

"The kind of work we do does not make us holy," wrote Meister Eckhart, "but we may make it holy."

So I look at the saints and wonder if we folks in the twenty-first century can still be like them. Can we be like St. Teresa in the sixteenth century, who found God among the pots and pans, or Brother Lawrence in the seventeenth who looked at his kitchen and saw a chapel, or Thérèse of Lisieux in the nineteenth who said (before any twentieth-century New Ager), "Each small task of everyday life is part of the total harmony of the universe?" I think we can, sometimes—they did—but not all the time. Nobody's perfect, not even the saints. I love St. Thérèse when she writes in her diary that some of her colleagues drove her nuts.

I also love the Zen story of the two monks carrying empty buckets to the bottom of a hill, where they filled them with water at the stream. They carried the full buckets back up to the monastery, emptied them, and then went back down the hill for more. Up and down, all day long, carrying buckets of water and smiling as if they were walking two feet off the ground. A stranger passing by watched them, puzzled, and asked, "Why are you so happy?" One of the monks answered, "We are bringing buckets of water up to the monastery!"

What makes the difference between working with frustration and working with love?

Love comes when we least expect it, when we no longer identify ourselves with our jobs but lose ourselves in the sacrament of the moment. Suddenly, we are no longer a teacher but teaching, no longer a repairman but repairing, no longer a salesperson but providing, no longer an accountant but balancing, no longer a mom but nurturing, comforting, and healing. Isn't this what makes the difference—the awareness that it is no longer we who are doing the work but the Love within us that does its work (John 14:10)?

It's also important to understand that "we work for money but we live for God" (Thomas Hora). We work for money seven, eight, maybe fourteen hours a day to live a comfortable life and provide for others. We live for God twenty-four hours a day, no matter what our work is.

Catholics somehow got the idea that working for money is unholy even though Jesus said, "The laborer deserves to be paid" (Luke 10:7, NRSV). Many of the saints didn't need to work for money to provide shelter and food and a little bit more for themselves and their families. Many didn't even have spouses or children but lived in monastic communities. That culture is disappearing. If Brother Lawrence were alive today, he might be a chef in a Greek restaurant, and while he would still practice the presence of God, he would also be grateful for his unemployment insurance. If Thérèse of Lisieux were alive today, she might be the most-beloved caregiver in a nursing home, but she would also make sure the home offered health insurance. If Teresa of Ávila were here today, she could well be the president of her own corporation and a philanthropist, but prayer would still be the center of her life. "We work for money, we live for God." They are not mutually exclusive, and if we know what we are here for, we will know how to work.

We may even change our jobs, more than once. Or not.

Which brings us back to Artie and me. Years later, Artie, no longer married, returned to the priesthood. With his son.

I remember his first phone call from the rectory. "Hold on a second," he said. I heard background noise. "Place is going nuts," he said. "I've got the mover here and he's saying, 'Mister, sign this!' My son is yelling, 'Dad!' And the secretary says someone wants to see Father. This is going to be fun!"

On my fiftieth birthday Vickie and our two sons threw a surprise party for me. My Dad, my hero, flew in from Chicago to surprise me. Friends and loved ones filled our house. They asked me to give a speech. I said, "I think I finally know what I want to be when I grow up. What I am right now."

I don't always love doing what I do but that's because I'm still discovering who and what I really am and what I'm here for. I know the words. I'm learning the Answer.

24

The Papacy, or It's a Tough Job but Somebody's Got to Do It

It often happens that I wake up at night and begin to think about a serious problem and decide I must tell the Pope about it. Then I wake up completely and remember that I am the pope.
—POPE JOHN XXIII (1881–1963)

In the movie *Manhattan* Woody Allen advises a friend to do the right thing. His friend says, "You are so self-righteous. I mean, we're just people. We're just human beings. You think you're God!"

Allen shrugs and says, "I gotta model myself after *someone.*"

We all need role models. God is the best. It also helps to have role models in the world who remind us to do the right thing. When it works, the papacy does a good job of that.

Who doesn't remember Pope John Paul II cooing love syllables with the young people at Madison Square Garden and defeating communism in Poland with quiet diplomacy? Who can ever forget "Good Pope John," who before becoming John XXIII helped save thousands of Jews from the Nazis and later opened the windows of the church as if they were eyes taking in the world for the first time. You probably don't know Pope Gregory the Great (c. 540–604), but when the hierarchy was even less credible than it is today, he insisted that bishops be first and foremost "physicians of the soul" and order their lives from a spiritual point of view. Gregory was also the first pope to refer to himself not as "Supreme Pontiff" or "His Holiness" but as "servant of the servants of God." Gregory, John, and John Paul—they all knew: "Whosoever will be chief among you, let him be your servant" (Matthew 20:27, KJV).

Not all 265 popes since Peter were role models. The papacy is like a net of fish: you never know what you're going to catch. In Morris West's novel *Lazarus* a character muses about the history of the popes: "Saints and sinners, wise men and fools, ruffians, rogues, reformers, and even an occasional madman! When they are gone, they are added to the list which began with Peter the Fisherman. The good are venerated; the bad are ignored. But the Church goes on."

Indeed it does, and let's face it: most people today don't know anything about anybody, good or bad, who hasn't been famous during the past three days (cf. Jay Leno, Jaywalking.). Take the bad popes (please). Does anyone remember Pope Paul III (1468–1549), who murdered his mother for her inheritance, resolved a theological dispute between bishops by having them hacked to death, and took over the prostitution business so he could get a piece of the pie? Now there's a man who knew how to balance a budget. Do you know who the second pope was? His name was Linus, and he didn't drag around a blankie; that was another Linus. Truth is, most Americans wouldn't know that John Adams was the second president if it weren't for HBO. Do you know who Paul Giamatti is? You're ahead of the curve.

When the topic of the papacy comes up for academic debate, the key issue is whether or not the pope is infallible. One person says, "All the popes are descended from Peter, who was given the keys to the kingdom of heaven, and that is why they are infallible." Another responds, "Only God is infallible." They usually don't have much to say after that. Truth is, the doctrine of infallibility wasn't even declared until 1870 at the First Vatican Council, and it has conditions attached to it under the rubric of *ex cathedra*, which renders it rare at best. Since 1870 there has been only *one* infallible statement *ex cathedra*: the Assumption of Mary in 1950, and one declared *ex cathedra in retro*, the Immaculate Conception in 1854. Catholics celebrate the Feast of the Immaculate Conception every December 8th and, if you are an average Catholic, chances are fifty-fifty that you know what it means. It refers not to the conception of Jesus but to the conception of Mary.

The issue of infallibility is not a topic of interest for Catholics. No one goes to bed at night worrying about it. It rarely comes up in conversations. What comes up are the same kinds of questions people pose about all religious leaders: "How is he doing? Is he a holy man? What is he doing to help us want to be more like Christ and love our neighbors as ourselves?"

The pope represents 1.3 billion Catholics. The whole world is interested in what he says and does. Basketball star LeBron James gets less attention. It's a tough job, but somebody's got to do it.

And when it works, it's so beautiful. When John Paul II, seeking to heal centuries of misunderstanding between Christians and Jews, visited Auschwitz and became the first pope to pray in a synagogue, he began a new chapter in religious history. When Paul VI went to the UN in the midst of the Vietnam War to declare, "No more war, war never again! One cannot love with offensive weapons in his hands!" he challenged every world leader to seek peace. When Pius XII during World War II helped save more than eight hundred thousand Jews from death through public appeals, hidden sanctuaries, ransom monies, emergency passports, fake baptismal certificates, and diplomatic maneuverings—despite his critics' claims that he should have done more—he fulfilled the Talmud injunction "Whoever saves a life, it is considered as if he saved an entire world!"

That's what a pope is: the servant of the servants of God. It is a wonderful job.

And—did you know this?—any Catholic can be elected pope.

A few years ago, as the cardinals were soon to elect a pope to follow John Paul II, the e-zine *Just Good Company*, just for good fun, asked me to write a brief essay on what I would do if I were pope. I wrote it in one fell swoop and was amazed to see it go viral throughout the U.S. and as far as Europe and Australia. I include it now just in case a lot of cardinals read this book and are so taken by it they'd like to send my name up in white smoke the next time. I'm only seventy; it could happen.

> If I were Pope I'd have a ball. I'd be "Happy Pope," and smile a lot. I'd stand on the balcony and stretch out my arms in a great embrace and tell everyone I love them and, even better, God loves them, no matter what. I'd tell everybody wherever I went that nothing can separate them from the love of God, not death, not sin, not anyone or anything. I'd tell that to my worker bees in the Curia before reducing it by half and encouraging every priest under sixty to join the missions. I'd tell that to sinners, saints, and fools, to liberals, conservatives, and confused, to Catholics, Protestants, Muslims, and Jews. I'd preach God's unconditional love to God's children in every country, to those with AIDS in Africa, to those in prisons and in hospitals, to those who are divorced and remarried, to everybody everywhere. They would know that I meant it, and that it was true, even if it was hard for them to believe. Someday, if I said it well enough and often enough, and most of all proved it with my life, other leaders in the church would do it too, and the children of God wouldn't have to believe—they would know. I can't wait to be Pope! I'll live in the Vatican two months a year to catch up on paperwork, but the rest of the year I'll live in parishes throughout the world— the one by Cabrini Green in Chicago, the one under suspicion in Beijing, the one high in the Alto Plano of

Peru. I'll be like Henry Fonda in *The Grapes of Wrath*: "A fellow ain't got a soul of his own, just a little piece of a big soul, the one big soul that belongs to everybody, so I'll be everywhere, wherever you can look. Wherever there's a fight so hungry people can eat, I'll be there. Wherever there's a cop beatin' up a guy, I'll be there. I'll be in the way guys yell when they're mad. I'll be in the way kids laugh when they're hungry and they know supper's ready, and where people are eatin' the stuff they raise and livin' in the houses they build. I'll be there too!" Yup, that's where I'll be when I'm Pope. I'll be in Israel and Palestine, in Bosnia and Afghanistan; I'll sleep in a favela in Brazil, a high-rise in Manhattan, and a houseboat in the bay of Hong Kong. And wherever I am, I'll preach nothing more and nothing less than the incredible, overwhelming love of God that is closer to us than breathing, and nearer than hands and feet. I'd like to write more about when I'm Pope but I've got to go now and practice my embrace. The way I see it, even if I don't get to be Pope, it's important to become that kind of person wherever and whatever I happen to be.

25

The Best Is Yet to Come

*No eye has seen, no ear has heard, and no
mind has imagined the things that God has
prepared for those who love him.*
—1 CORINTHIANS 2:9, GOD'S WORD TRANSLATION

See, I am making all things new.
—REVELATION 21:5, NRSV

You ain't seen nuthin' yet!
—JIMMY DURANTE

When Vickie and I first met, I asked her, "What is your
philosophy of life?" She said without hesitation, "Life is
for shit."

"How can you say that?" I said. "You're a happy, cheer-
ful person."

"You see my eye," she said. Her right eye was scarred
and cloudy, the color of a sea shell. When she was fifteen
months old, Vickie fell on a glass Easter rabbit and was
blinded in that eye. "When I was a little girl, I walked
with my face down so people wouldn't see how ugly I was.

Sometimes people, even strangers, asked me embarrassing questions or made hurtful remarks. When the kids played games, I was always the monster. I grew up imagining that everyone looked at me with disdain, as if the way I looked was my fault. I was a freak. Life was for shit. Thank God there was a heaven at the end."

"How did you get through the days?"

"Mama. She always said to me, 'Hold your head up high and face the world.' It became a litany that became a part of me. She would hold me in her arms and stroke my hair and say, 'If you hold your head up high, it will be okay, and people will see your beautiful soul.' She said it again and again. She said it whenever I wanted to hide. When I was in high school, I was popular and got all A's. I was even elected class president, but I still felt like a freak. All I wanted was to look like everybody else. When things got really bad, I would cry to Mama, and she would look at me with her loving eyes and say, 'Hold your head up high and face the world. Let them see the beauty inside.'"

I told her the truth: she was just as beautiful on the *outside.*

She knew I meant it. "What is your philosophy of life?" she asked.

"That heaven begins right here. We couldn't be further apart. Yet I walk around with a sadness in my heart. And you walk around glowing, with your head held high. What gives?"

One year later we were married.

A month after we wed, Vickie's bad eye got infected. It had to be removed. She received an artificial eye that was soft and green, just like her good one. She now looked like everybody else.

Forty-one years later Vickie still believes that life is for shit, but she also knows that heaven does begin right here. I still believe that heaven begins right here but have also come to accept that life is for shit. We both walk with our heads held high and smile a lot.

Both sides are true.

Catholicism promises us that after we die we will see Beauty that eyes cannot see. We will hear Music that ears cannot hear. We will know Love that no mind can imagine.

And it all begins right here, on the spot where we are standing. Like Moses and Isaiah, whether we know it or not, "we are standing on holy ground" (Exodus 3:5).

Life on earth is hard and often cruel, but—thank God—God is not only Abba (Daddy) but Mama and Mamma Lou, caressing us, comforting us, holding us, telling us how beautiful we are, no matter how things look or what people think. When Jesus looked over the city of Jerusalem, he said, "How often have I wanted to gather your children as a mother hen gathers her brood under her wings!" Pope John Paul II compared God's love to the love that only a mother can give: "tender, merciful, patient, and full of understanding." When life on earth is for shit, and it often is, God hugs us and holds us in her arms and inspires us to hold our head up high. And she promises to make all things new.

Vickie and I talk about heaven sometimes, and again we couldn't be further apart. I think what is good and beautiful and true in us continues without interruption, but I can't imagine what it is like. Vickie is specific. She envisions a beatific vision that is like being in a great big show with all your loved ones and watching a movie on a huge screen.

"But that would be boring," I tell her.

"No," she assures me. "It's the beatific vision."

So I ask her, "Okay, if you get there first, order a big recliner for me. I can already see Mama Lou on her big blue sofa and Mama next to you in her big easy chair and you on a comfy overstuffed chair too, but I see a hard folding chair on your right waiting for me. Please ask God for a recliner, like the one in the family room, okay?"

"I will."

Nobody knows what life after death will be like. But I know it will be.

I am still Catholic because heaven makes perfect sense.

PART 2

People

Ideas are energy and, according to physicist Werner Heisenberg, "Energy can be neither created nor destroyed but only transmuted into other forms." The energy of ideas expresses itself in people and manifests in places. Here are a few people whom I think express some of the spiritual qualities of the eternal Word: love, creativity, gratitude, compassion, peace, and joy. They are exemplars of Catholic ideas—and are among the best reasons I can think of for staying in the church.

Miriam Therese Winter

26

The Singer and the Song: Miriam Therese Winter

God of my childhood
and my call,
make me a window, not a wall,
So like an icon,
may I be a sign of love's transparency,
and through the love that lives in me,
proclaim your lasting love for all.
—MIRIAM THERESE WINTER, FROM HER SONG
"GOD OF MY CHILDHOOD"

Miriam Therese Winter taught me to go to church like a woman. I've had a hard time listening to sermons ever since.

M. T. Winter is one of the most alive Catholic role models I've ever known. She has served God and the poor on three continents. She is the composer of sixteen recordings, including the gold record album *Joy Is Like the Rain*. A Medical Mission sister, M. T. is professor of liturgy, worship, and spirituality at Hartford Seminary, Hartford, Connecticut. She is the author of sixteen books, including *The Gospel According to Mary, Paradoxology,* and *eucharist with a small e.*

M. T. is one of 750,000 sisters throughout the world. Many Catholics believe that if religious women were in charge of the church, the world would be a better place.

I've had the pleasure of being M. T.'s editor and publisher for many years. I remember one evening driving up to Hartford Seminary for an autograph party. After the celebration I joined her and M. E. (Sister Mary Elizabeth) at the seminary cottage they call home. It's also a temporary shelter for stray animals and stray people, some from a nearby prison where M. T. counsels inmates, and is as comfortable as a big, fat sofa. Books were bursting out of the shelves and piled high here and there on the floor, like weapons of mass instruction. An old piano with chipped keys sat in the screened-in porch, like an old friend who was as happy as a songbird to be there. M. T., M. E., and I sat in the tiny kitchen over cups of hot tea and talked long into the night.

I opened my heart (that's what friends do in a small kitchen when it's late and the window is black). It was around the time my wife, my sweetheart, Vickie, had been diagnosed with Alzheimer's, and we were scared. I'll always remember how M. T. listened. I can't remember what she said, but I'll always remember how present she was. A good friend turns up the light in a dark room.

When I drove back home, colorful epiphanies appeared. The color orange kept smiling at me. Did I tell you that I had a shiny, orange roller-skate case when I was twelve and how much it meant to me? Those were blithe times, skating after school in St. Andrew's gym with pretty seventh-grade girls, sometimes even an eighth grader. Orange is my favorite color.

So there I was, driving down I-95 in Connecticut, and billboards with orange colors kept appearing off the road, and orange safety cones grew out of the strip like metal flowers, and bright orange trucks were passing me by. One orange-colored truck passed and got in front of me. It moved slowly but I didn't want to pass it. My eyes opened wide. The truck had a sign on its back with a slogan that warmed me with peace. I don't remember what the slogan said. I do remember that it was prosaic, but to me it was better than Shakespeare: the concise words supported what M. T. had been saying to me and were words I needed to hear at that moment. I followed it all the way home. Thanks, M. T.

Did I tell you about the time that M. T. was scheduled to be the keynote speaker at a big Catholic convention? A thousand people had signed up months in advance to hear her. Shortly before the event, an X-ray revealed that M. T. had breast cancer. She was fearful. She was also faithful. M. T. had her breast removed, and three weeks later flew to the conference and gave one of the most inspiring talks on the love of God I have ever heard. I think the people are still applauding.

Here is M. T. in her own words, from her memoir *The Singer and the Song*:

Another day. Another long, hot, hard, exhausting, exasperating day in Ethiopia. Well, better one day in Your tent, O God, O suffering, saving, compassionate God, than a thousand in the security of my own home in Connecticut. It is time to celebrate the "liturgy" for which I was ordained. I pull on my jeans and my thick-soled shoes. God, I believe, help my unbelief. God, let all that I do praise you.

It is just after dawn and already the long, brown, deathly silent line snakes all around the perimeter of our camp and loses itself in the distance. Our intense feeding center for emaciated children is a temporary refuge. Daily, every two hours, what serves as bread is figuratively blessed, broken, and distributed under a variety of disguises: soybean porridge or hotcake; high protein biscuits; thick, sweet powdered milk laced with oil and sugar; and once in a while, God be praised, a very, very small banana.

Seven times a day I take, break, bless, distribute, and all around give thanks as the Author of life restores to life those physically diminished. Seven times a day, a miracle, when fully present to the Presence, I can see the shape of grace. It is 10 A.M., time once again for me to fulfill my primary daily function, presiding over a "liturgy of the eucharist," presiding over the distribution of desperately needed "daily bread." When you see a hungry person and feed that person, you are feeding me, said Jesus. I look out over the beautiful brown faces of my sisters and brothers, broken bodies with unbroken spirits. This is my body, said Jesus. Amen, I say. Amen.

Come and see: mtwinter.hartsem.edu and medicalmissionsisters.org

Mitch Finley

27

Poet Laureate of Catholicism: Mitch Finley

Catholic joy comes from knowing that in the long run and the short run there is no need to be afraid or anxious because no matter what happens, good or bad, God's love for us is absolutely reliable, more trustworthy than the best things that can happen to us, and more powerful than the worst things that can happen to us. Even death.
—MITCH FINLEY, *THE JOY OF BEING CATHOLIC*

When he was in third grade at Sts. Peter and Paul in Grangeville, Idaho, Mitch Finley raised his hand high when Fr. Lafey asked the boys if they wanted to be priests. That was a bold move for a boy who wasn't even Catholic. It was even bolder when Mitch converted to Catholicism at nine, fell in love with Catholic community at De Sales High School in Walla Walla, Washington, earned an MA in theology at Marquette University, and then—did *not* become a priest. Instead he married Kathy and went on to write thirty books about Catholicism that have instructed and inspired Catholics for four decades. Even though he doesn't write poetry, one reviewer dubbed Mitch "the poet laureate of Catholicism."

Mitch's books and articles have received many honors and awards, including eleven Catholic Press Association Awards and an Excellence in Writing Award from the prestigious American Society of Journalists and Authors. He taught theology at Gonzaga University for a while and could have written scholarly books but chose instead, like his hero Andrew Greeley, to write for people in the pews. Mitch has a sign on his desk that reads: "True originality lies not in saying what has never been said, but in saying what you have to say."

You won't find Mitch's books reviewed in the *New York Times* Book Review, and you won't see him interviewed on *Entertainment Tonight*. But you may see people reading his books on busses, and if you're ever walking down Gordon Avenue in Spokane, you might catch him playing his banjo on his porch across the street from a city park. For Mitch, the five-string banjo is part of "the joy of being Catholic."

"Banjo time has become, for me, a time of grace," writes Mitch in *Santa Clara* magazine. "Resurrection to new life can happen even with—truly, because I have— a banjo in my hands. Even a banjo can become part of a sacramental spirituality, a conduit of God's divine life channeled to the human heart through everyday things: the sacred in the ordinary."

The banjo was another entry for Mitch into the sacramental imagination. "I was watching performances of great banjo players, each with a unique style, and these happy pickers became metaphors or images of God for me: a playful, graceful, humorous God. I couldn't help but smile. This, too, is what God is like!"

The Finley two-story, three-bedroom home in Spokane is the home of the average American. Photos hang on the refrigerator door, including one of a family the Finleys support in Guatemala through Family-to-Family, a local organization. Mitch and Kathy like to eat in the kitchen and always say grace, just as they did with their boys when they ate as a family. They are empty nesters now. They like it.

Mitch is not the only Finley who writes. Kathy's book *The Liturgy of Motherhood* was a Catholic Press Association Book Award-winner. The Finleys don't watch much TV. They read like crazy. And are very best friends.

I could quote here from any number of Mitch's books, but since the purpose of this book is to respond to the question *Why Stay Catholic?* I asked Mitch to share the core ideas that sustain him. Here they are. Thanks, Mitch!

When I was an undergraduate at Santa Clara University, in California, back in the late 1960s and early '70s, I majored in Religious Studies. While I am proud to be a Santa Clara alum and grateful for the excellent education I received, there are few specific ideas I can recall at will from all that I learned during those years. A few do remain with me, however, such as: The only valid way to evaluate any human institution, organization, or association is to evaluate the most basic principles, ideals, and goals upon which that institution, organization, or association is founded.

This idea may not sound particularly exciting, but it's quite common for people to base their evaluations on other things.

It's common, for example, for people to choose a church or religious tradition based on how warm and welcoming they experience the community they find in that church or religious tradition to be. Many people, if asked why they belong to a particular church, say that they "feel at home" there. Others, when explaining why they left a particular religion, say that they did so because they were scandalized by the behavior of the clergy or some of the people in that church. Directly to the point of this book, there are a good many inactive Catholics or people who call themselves ex-Catholics who "left" because of the clergy sex abuse scandal, and sometimes the leadership failures, that generated so much media attention during the early years of the twenty-first century.

While the decision to take one's leave of any institution, organization, or association for such reasons is surely understandable, it can also be unrealistic to the point of naíveté. This is so because the only assumption upon which this departure can be based is that the leaders and/or people in this group or institution must always act in ways that measure up to my personal understanding of perfection. Closely related to this assumption is the implication that I, myself, always live up to my personal ideals and beliefs. Therefore, being perfect and without sin myself, I may judge and condemn those whose sins and failures have scandalized me to the point that I will no longer have anything to do with the group, association, or church to which I formerly belonged.

The only way to avoid placing oneself in this absurd situation is to choose to evaluate no group, church, institution, or association except according to its ultimate ideals, principles, and goals. It simply will never work to base an evaluation on how success-fully the people in that church or group actually live up to their most basic ideals and principles, because they will *never* do so. Never. It makes more sense, for example, to keep track of how *often* Catholics, and Catholic institutions and groups, *do* live up to the ideals they profess. It happens quite frequently!

An extreme example: I may come across a warm, friendly, welcoming group. Gosh, they're swell people, so friendly and so much fun. The only prob-lem is that they happen to be neo-Nazi white suprem-acists. Oops. No matter what a friendly, fun-loving group of folks they are, I can never accept their most basic ideals and principles.

What about the most basic ideals and principles of the church called Catholic? There are more than a few, and it's not easy to express any of them briefly. Still, in no particular order, herewith a few:

✛ The ultimate and most immediate meaning and purpose of life is found nowhere but in the every-day love of God—who is above all our loving Father and Mother who is closer to us than we are to ourselves—and the people we live and work with most closely.

✛ Scripture cannot be separated from its source, the Christian community's 2000-year-old, here-and-now, ongoing experience of the risen Christ (Sacred Tradition).

✛ The church, meaning all the baptized, is gifted with seven Sacraments, tangible signs and carriers of the invisible, real, nourishing, healing love of Christ. (A related principle: the sacred is in the ordinary.)

✛ The church, the People of God, is a community that transcends and exists in both time and eternity, and we participate in this community even now.

✛ All this, and so much more, means that you'll never find me anyplace but in the one, holy, catholic, apostolic, knockabout, utterly imperfect, sometimes shamefully sinful, regularly frustrating, always joy-evoking, grace-filled Catholic Church.

Come and see: www.mitchandkathyfinley.com

Thea Bowman

28

She Who Overcame: Thea Bowman

*I can't preach in the church. Women can't preach in the
Catholic Church. But I can preach in the streets. I can
preach in the neighborhood. I can preach in the home.
I can teach and preach in the family.*
—THEA BOWMAN (1937–1990)

Let's pay less attention to scandalous priests and athletes
and politicians and turn our attention to role models who
not only never let us down but lift everybody up. Sister
Thea Bowman died in 1990, yet she still astonishes us. You
don't know much about her? That's okay—that's why she's
here. Let me introduce you.

Born in Mississippi in 1937, Thea Bowman learned to
love Jesus as a child and entered a Franciscan convent of
white nuns in Wisconsin when she was seventeen. Without
seeking it, Thea would become a pioneer role model in
interracial relations. What did she do? She did what she
was told. But wherever she went, Thea expressed what she
knew: God's transforming love. "Sometimes people think

they have to do big things in order to make change," Thea said, "but if each one would light a candle, we'd have a tremendous light. My goal is to share good news. I want people to know that happiness is possible."

People caught happiness just by being near her.

Thea's great-grandparents were freed slaves. She was proud to be African American. While she earned a PhD in English literature and was an expert on William Faulkner, Thea was known most of all as a gifted singer and speaker. Her voice and presence were unforgettable, whether she was filling a Mississippi church as a teenager or echoing through a Northern cathedral packed with people of all races when she was an adult. While she helped found the prestigious Institute for Black Catholic Studies at Xavier University in New Orleans, Thea came to national attention by preaching the gospel to parishes throughout the United States. She inspired Mike Wallace in the most repeated *60 Minutes* interview of all time, was sought out by Muhammad Ali, Harry Belafonte, and Whoopi Goldberg, and finally, stricken with bone cancer, led in the singing of "We Shall Overcome" in the halls of the U.S. Catholic bishops, inspiring those stodgy men to stand up and sing, to clap and sway in the name of the Lord!

It was at that remarkable meeting in 1989, just months before her death, that Thea, bent over in a wheelchair on a stage that happened to be higher than the assembled bishops, challenged them: "What does it mean to be black in the church and society?"

She answered by sitting tall and singing, "Sometimes I Feel Like a Motherless Child." Her voice broke through walls. "Can you hear me, church? Will you help me, church? I'm a long way from home, a long way from my home." She asked again, "What does it mean to be black and Catholic? It means that I come to my church fully functioning. That doesn't frighten you, does it? I bring myself, my black self, all that I am, all that I have, all that I hope to become. I bring my whole history, my traditions, my experience, my culture, my African-American song and dance and gesture and movement and teaching and preaching and healing and responsibility as gift to the church!"

At the end, as Thea was wheeled down the aisle of the auditorium, the bishops got out of their seats and lined up against the wall to witness her passing. Some of them knelt at her wheelchair. Many embraced her. All were silent.

After a long illness, Thea Bowman died at age fifty-three.

It is a mystery that a life that shone like a billion candles could flicker out so soon. Yet that is a key aspect of Thea's journey. She was a woman who showed us how to drink deeply of life's cup to the very end, even as she spent her last years in pain.

"When I first found out I had cancer," Thea told an interviewer from *Praying*, "I didn't know what to pray for. I didn't know if I should pray for healing or life or death. Then I found peace in praying for what my folks call 'God's perfect will.' As it evolved my prayer has become,

'Lord, let me live until I die.' By that I mean I want to live, love, and serve fully until death comes. If that prayer is answered, how long really doesn't matter. Whether it's just a few months or a few years is really immaterial." When the interviewer asked her if God was really present in suffering, Thea answered:

> God is present in everything. In the universe, in creation, in me and all that happens to me, in my brothers and sisters, in the church—everywhere. In the midst of suffering, I feel God's presence and cry out to God for help, "Lord, help me to hold on!" I don't try to make sense of suffering. I try to make sense of life. I try to keep myself open to people and to laughter and to love and to have faith. I try each day to see God's will. I pray, "Oh Jesus, I surrender." I pray, "Father, take this cross away. Not my will, but thy will be done." I console myself with the old Negro spiritual, "Soon I will be done with the troubles of this world. I'm going home to live with God!"

Everyone wanted to be near Thea Bowman. They soaked up her joy like a sponge fills with water. She changed the way people thought about themselves. Her example was an antidote to prejudice, exclusion, sadness, and all the things that drive people apart. "If we are not family," she taught, "we can't become church." Thea Bowman didn't live for the church, or for herself, or for others. She lived for God. Her life tells us what it means to belong to the family of God.

Come and see: www.fspa.org (About Us/Thea Bowman) and *Thea's Song: The Life of Thea Bowman* by Charlene Smith and John Feister

Pat Reardon

29

Friend of Those Who Have No Friend: Pat Reardon

And finally, I ask of you all, become friends to those who have no friends. Become family to those who have no family. And become community to those who have no community.
—POPE JOHN PAUL II

Boston Blackie was a cool private eye in a series of old black-and-white movies. He was charming and dangerous. The narrator introduced Blackie as "an enemy of those who make him an enemy, a friend of those who have no friend." Let me tell you something: Blackie had nothing on Pat Reardon of Chicago. Pat is a fearless criminal defense attorney who has helped people in dangerous situations that Blackie would run away from in a Boston second.

Pat, a former Catholic priest who served in a poor parish until his midthirties, is currently first assistant public defender of Cook County. He directs a staff of five hundred lawyers who defend the indigent against criminal accusations. "We do this for the same reason Atticus Finch did what he did," says Pat. "It's the right thing to do."

Pat and I have been friends for fifty years. When he was a teenager, Pat looked like a nerd, with his lanky frame, unruly blond hair, and oversized glasses. Actually he looks pretty much the same today. But pity those who messed with him then, and pity those who would mess with him now. I remember when Pat was sixteen, on a dare he climbed up the bricks of a three-story apartment building, all the way to the roof. He looked down at us from the top and laughed like he had just raised a flag on Mount Everest. He must have felt that way, too, when he defended his first case in front of the Supreme Court. "It was an honor just to be in the same room with Thurgood Marshall," he remembers. "The kindest man I ever knew."

Pat believes with all his heart that the least of us deserves to be heard when accused of a crime. He has defended thousands of people over the past thirty years: alleged murderers like Barabbas, thieves like those who hung on either side of Jesus, and scapegoats like Jesus, whose only counsel was his Father in heaven. If Pat were on a jury instead of in front of one, he'd be Henry Fonda from *Twelve Angry Men*. Pat recalls walking out of a dingy criminal court one afternoon with his seventeen-year-old client Juan. He had put Juan on the stand. A policeman then testified in contradiction to everything the young man said. After Pat's cross-examination, the judge ruled in favor of Juan.

In the hallway, Juan turned to Pat and said, "Mr. Reardon, I was under oath on that stand, right?"

"Yes," Pat said.

"That meant I had to tell the honest truth."

"Yes," said Pat, "and you did."

"Mr. Reardon, didn't that witness take the same oath?"

Pat had no answer for his innocent client, then or now, except to say how much he appreciates giving a kid with no hope a chance to be believed when he swears to tell the truth. "People seek my help when all have turned against them," Pat says, "and they feel the withering stares of accusation and the self-doubt such looks breed. Jesus said, 'The last shall be first.' I like being able to walk with those on the bottom into the highest forums in the land and demand that they be presumed innocent, as is their right."

As far back as I can remember, Pat has had compassion for the underdog and has been friendly with everyone, especially those other people shun. Where did that come from? "I grew up in a house that welcomed the stranger," Pat says. "At various times my mother and father hosted refugees from the Hungarian revolution, an exiled Cuban girl, a French choir singer, and countless others. Some stayed a few days or weeks; Hartmut, a German high school student, stayed almost a year. My four siblings and I always felt free to invite friends. My mother still talks about coming down to the kitchen in the morning to find a completely unknown teenager looking through the refrigerator and saying, 'Mrs. Reardon, you're out of milk.'

"That home shaped my vision of the word *Catholic*. A church that dares to call itself by that name must throw open its doors, its windows, its attics, and its refrigerators for all. Catholic means everyone is worthwhile, everyone belongs. There are no exceptions."

For the past twenty years Pat has been representing clerics and religious of various faiths who have failed in their ministry. He takes cases other attorneys won't touch, and often does it for free. "I've witnessed the confusion and agony of men and women coming to realize that they have been professing a public vision in painful contradiction to the lives they led, mired in addictions to drugs, sex, or personal greed. I have shared their sadness when they realized they were no longer welcome in the church they had once committed to serve. I have also shared the rage of the many falsely accused Catholic priests when they found that the church they had faithfully served appeared to reject their word and presume guilt unless they could independently prove that their accuser was lying."

Pat defended one priest who was removed from his parish on the accusation of a woman who claimed he had sexually abused her on a desk in a classroom while a nun in the back strummed a guitar and sang "Kumbaya." Pat proved his innocence. It was too late. The priest's reputation was ruined, and now he lives in a rural area far away from the diocese. Pat visits him, just as he did the prisoners in jail he had represented.

Pat Reardon knows that Jesus died for all of us, *really*. He has his parent's vision of Catholicism. He is a friend to those who have no friend, a family to those who have no family, a community for those who have no community. He has seen his church's best side and its worst side. "I have been at times a priest, lawyer, husband, father, sinner. I stay Catholic even though I sometimes don't recognize the church into which I was once ordained. I am embarrassed by many of the policies and statements from many priests and bishops. I frequently wonder why I bother to continue attending Mass when I feel such little kinship with church leaders. I guess it is just hard to shake off my vision that God's is a welcoming house. As long as I am still welcome, I will still come."

Bob McCahill

30

The Muslim's Neighbor: Bob McCahill

Where I am, there will my servant be also.
—JOHN 12:26, NRSV

Bob McCahill, aka The Bicycle Disciple, is a Maryknoll missioner who has spent the past thirty-five years of his life serving the poor in Bangladesh. Fr. McCahill hails from Indiana, but he's been in the Far East so long he is starting to look like Mohandas Gandhi. Short, wiry, and tan, the seventy-three-year-old missionary still pedals his bike from village to village, visiting the sick, and once a week escorting them on a beat-up bus to the hospital in Dhaka where he arranges for free care.

Brother Bob never tries to convert people. "My mission is to show the love of Christ," he says, "the love of God for all people of all faiths, to be with them as a brother, to establish brotherhood by being a brother to them." He lives in a small hut in the midst of his Muslim neighbors.

He says Mass in the morning and welcomes anyone who wishes to come. He chats with men in the tea shops where they congregate, banters with merchants at the bazaar, pumps water for children, cooks on a one-burner kerosene stove, and most of all rides his bike along those dusty roads in search of the sick, offering them and their families hope and help. When people ask, "Who are you? Why do you do what you are doing?" he answers:

"I am your Christian brother. I go about doing good and healing because that is what Jesus did. Jesus is my model. I am his follower."

Some people call that interreligious dialogue. Catholics call it mission. Fr. Bob McCahill calls it his vocation. He is a role model not only for Catholics but for people of all faiths. Here is more of "the Muslim's Neighbor," in his own words:

> One evening I returned home by bus, having admitted a few children to Dhaka hospitals. Rain was falling as I began my walk to the hut in the dark. Within minutes I felt a sharp bite on my foot. I flashed my light and saw a snake slithering away.
>
> You could say I was worried. Over 6000 people die from snakebites each year in Bangladesh. So I decided to call on my neighbor. When Alom realized the danger, he started to pray out loud, applying pressure to my foot. Then Kobad arrived on the scene and applied pressure, too, starting at my head and working down to the snakebite. In the morning Alom came

to check on me. "Still living," I assured him. "By the grace of the Almighty," he declared.

Worrying over snakebites isn't the only thing that will disturb your sleep in Bangladesh. For all its beauty, it is a country continually struggling for survival. Almost 156 million people—about the size of Iowa. Close to half of them live in poverty, and children are malnourished. Many have birth defects. With personal income about $1.25 a day, you can see the consequences of poverty without trying hard.

For more than 30 years, my mission here has been simple: I live the way Jesus did, caring for the poor. I take children to the hospital for evaluations and surgeries. I visit the homebound to make sure they are taking their medicines and do not feel alone. I write letters for women who find certain conversations too difficult to have with their doctors. I help patients with paperwork they don't understand. The wonderful thing about my mission is that once someone knows what I do, they tell a neighbor. A farmer ran from his rice field one day to stop me as I was passing by, obviously aware of my work. He said a child needed surgery, and inquired if I could help.

I explained that I am a Christian missionary. "If you are a Christian," he asked, "why would you help a Muslim?" I told him that as long as we are serving one another, we are serving God."

I was able to reinforce this point one day at a tea stall where men gather for serious conversation.

Janhangir and his friends wanted to know more about my faith. So I told them. After listening, Janhangir said how fortunate he felt to know why I live among them— because of the life and teachings of Jesus.

Come and see: maryknoll.org and *Dialogue of Life: A Christian among Allah's Poor* by Bob McCahill

Tom Kaminski

31

Upon This Rock I Will Build My Church: Tom Kaminski

You are Peter, and on this rock I will build my church.
—Matthew 16:18, NRSV

If it weren't for the Kaminskis of Catholicism there would be no church. A parish priest for more than forty-five years, Fr. Tom Kaminski finally had to leave his ministry because of lung cancer. While many priests have a summer home to retire to or can afford a condo when they hit seventy, the Rock, as he is known, may eventually live at the Bishop Lyne Home for Priests in Lemont, Illinois, far from his beloved St. Helen of the Cross on the South Side of Chicago. Rock didn't come from money, never had money, and spent much of his meager salary on others.

If he could, he would die in an unmade bed in a rectory after another fourteen-hour day. "I'd like to live in another rectory so I could help out," he says, "as long as I'm not a burden on another pastor."

St. Jean Vianney (1786–1859) is the patron saint of parish priests. The *Catholic Encyclopedia* lists his miracles and concludes: "The greatest miracle of all was his life. He worked incessantly with unfailing humility, gentleness, patience, and cheerfulness." It could be an entry for the Rock.

St. Peter got his nickname "Rock" from Jesus. Tom Kaminski got his from his fourteen-year-old classmates at Quigley Preparatory Seminary in 1955. He told us that *Kamin* in Polish meant "rock." That was it. The Rock never failed to live up to his name. Some of us think Sly Stallone named his first hero after our guy.

Rock Kaminski wasn't the smartest amongst us, or the best athlete, or among the most popular. He was the hardest worker, the most dedicated, and among the most authentic. When thinking of him, I always hear these lines from the musical *The King and I*:

This is a man who thinks with his heart,
His heart is not always wise.
This is a man who stumbles and falls,
But this is a man who tries.

It's conventional wisdom that nobody tried harder than the first Rock, Petros. Peter saw Jesus walking on water and leapt out of his boat to walk toward him. He sunk like a crosier. If he were the second Rock, Rock Kaminski, he would have tried to climb back on top of the water and walk toward Jesus again. The first Rock always thought with his heart. When Jesus washed his disciples' feet at the Last Supper, Peter refused, feeling unworthy. After Jesus insisted, Peter cried out, "Lord, not only my feet, but also my hands and my head!" The second Rock would have had half his clothes off by then. The first Rock denied Jesus three times and after Jesus' resurrection exclaimed his love three times. Double it for our Rock. It is upon this kind of Rock—human, humble, and heartfelt—that Jesus chose to build his church.

Fr. Kaminski will be the first to tell you that over the years he has worried too much, smoked too much, and sometimes drunk too much. He says, "I spend much of my time just surrendering to God's will." He takes pride in only one thing: "I am comfortable with others taking leadership. In my ministry I've focused on training all kinds of laypeople to do ministry. I am known for that." How many pastors would name empowering others as their number one accomplishment?

Many of us know the famous Mel Brooks line: "It's good to be the king!" But we could also say, "It's not so good to be the pastor." No matter what you do, somebody is going to be mad. In any job most of the problems that keep us awake at night have to do with people. So you can imagine what it's like to be a priest and endeavor to live for God and try to do the right thing and hear complaints from every side of every issue and begin to doubt yourself, as Peter did, again and again. I don't know how priests do it. But Rock did it for almost half a century. So have hundreds of thousands of priests like him who have never made the newspapers because they never did anything bad or never did anything grand but simply did the best they could with all that God gave them. "All of me, why not take all of me?" could be their song. Everybody calls them Father, but nobody calls them up when they're gone.

Priests like Rock remind me of a scene in the movie *A Bronx Tale*. Robert De Niro plays a bus driver with a ten-year-old son who admires a neighborhood big shot more than he does his dad. The boy says to his father, "Sonny was right. The working man is a sucker." His father says, "Get up every day and work for a living! Let's see him try that! We'll see who's really tough. The working man is tough." Parish priests who get up every day for forty-five years and work for others without interest in recompense are the real heroes in the church.

"I believe God is gracious," says Fr. Kaminski. "No matter what it is that I must face or endure, God will not abandon me to face it alone. I have to remind myself that God is in charge, and that I am God's beloved child. I've always preached a God who delights in us and loves us. I even say that 'God is crazy about us.' I'm just now starting to realize that it's true for me as well as for everyone else. As hard as life can get, I don't think there is ever a moment when God is not thinking about us and not giving us blessings. Faith is about opening our eyes and appreciating [those blessings]. I don't think God judges us when our eyes are shut either. Catholicism says that no matter what happens, God is right here loving us. That's what it's about. That's what keeps me going."

"The Dude abides" in film, but in life the Rock perseveres. That is a very big deal. Let's give it up for the Rocks of the Catholic Church.

Therese Borchard

32

Wounded Healer: Therese Borchard

"Wounded" people are so much more fun to hang out with than "flawless" folks who deny their illnesses and object to prescriptions. Because, for the large part, we wounded know how to laugh. And what freedom and humility and community there is in that laughter.
—THERESE BORCHARD, *BEYOND BLUE*

My best friend is a blue-eyed blonde who is young enough to be my daughter. In fact she *is* the daughter Vickie and I never had. Therese Borchard is many things to many people: wife, mother, daughter, friend, and to thousands who suffer from depression, a fountain of hope. If there were a patron saint of the bipolar, it would be Therese. She lifts them up, calms their fears, and makes them laugh.

She has that effect on everyone.

I first met Therese in 1998 when she was an aspiring writer. We collaborated on a book called *I Like Being Catholic*. We quickly became friends and shared our stories.

Therese, like me, came from a broken home. She had been a teenage alcoholic who suffered from clinical depression and overachieved in everything she did. She was only twenty-eight when we met but had already written ten books. She hadn't touched a drink since college but was on Zoloft and Prozac for her depression. Her theme song could have been "laughing on the outside but crying on the inside." Wherever she went, Therese put on a happy face. People loved to be around her. She was sunshine, even when clouds passed over her light.

Therese and Eric would soon have two beautiful children, David and Katherine Rose, and make a loving home in Annapolis, Maryland. But no matter what medicines Therese took, or how many therapists she saw, or how long she prayed, or how hard she tried, her depression was a black hole so deep and terrifying that no one who hasn't been there can ever understand it. Only her family and friends knew just how overwhelming her pain was and how courageous she was. In August 2005 Therese became psychotic from an atomic cocktail of drugs a psychiatrist had served her. She crashed and burned. She recalls the morning Eric took her to Johns Hopkins Hospital:

> Fear consumed me.
> Until I saw Jesus.
> In the lobby was a ten-and-a-half foot tall marble statue of Jesus, his arms extended toward those in desperate need of healing. The inscription, written in capital letters on the pedestal, read: "Come unto me all ye that are weary and heavy laden, and I will give you rest."

I stood in front of Jesus for a while, tempted to touch his robe like the hemorrhaging woman who got her miracle in the gospels of Mark and Luke. She had bled for twelve years, "had endured much under many physicians, and had spent all that she had; and she was no better" (Mark 5:26). Just by touching the hem of Jesus' cloak, this ailing woman was healed of her disease, because her faith was so great.

"I believe, Jesus," I said to the statue, imagining myself touching the hem of Jesus' real robe, "I believe."

And I wept at his feet.

The doctors at Hopkins detoxed her, put her on a safe regimen, and with the help of a new psychiatrist, her family, and friends, Therese slowly climbed out of the rabbit hole. "Something must have happened the moment I wept at Jesus' feet in the lobby of Hopkins, when I told Jesus that I really did believe in miracles and I was in desperate need of one. Because I got one."

In 2006, Beliefnet.com, the popular religion Web site, asked Therese to write a daily blog on depression. Therese named it *Beyond Blue: A Spiritual Journey to Mental Health.* She wrote:

To most eyes I look normal, and I can behave normally, at least for two-hour intervals. No one would guess my insides to be so raw, or suspect that I was twice committed to a psych ward, was suicidal for close to two years, and considered ECT,

electroconvulsive therapy, after the first 22 medi-
cation combinations failed. Then again, the more
human beings I interview Barbara-Walters-style, the
more convinced I am that everyone struggles. There
are just many layers, varieties, and degrees of strains
inside the human psyche.

The only difference between me and most of the
civilized world is that they don't publish their insecuri-
ties, irrational fears, personality flaws, and embarrassing moments online and in print for everyone, including
their in-laws and neighbors, to read.

Why on earth would I do that?

It has something to do with the twelfth step of
most twelve-step support groups I've attended, which
is nearly all of them: to share my experience, strength
(if you can call it that), and hope with others in order
to secure some sanity for myself. Or, to use the language of existentialist Soren Kierkegaard, the twelfth
step is about getting cozy with our true selves, becoming "transparent under God," and vulnerable before
others in order to form a bond of communion with
those persons experiencing similar struggles.

Within months *Beyond Blue* was the most popular blog on
Beliefnet.

A year later, PsychCentral.com chose it as one of the
top ten depression blogs.

While it still appears every day on Beliefnet, *Beyond
Blue* is featured weekly on *The Huffington Post*. Therese has
become a go-to expert in the field of popular psychology.

Her work has been cited in major newspapers, magazines, and Web sites. She has been featured in *O* magazine, *Psychology Today, Parenting, More, Redbook, Ladies' Home Journal*, and the *Washington Post.*

But none of that is as important as the daily responses from people struggling with depression. Here is what *Beyond Blue* really means:

> Therese, you are my savior. I don't know how you continue to do it but you always speak to my heart. Every time I read your website posts the topic always applies to something I am going through right now. You are an amazing woman and are helping me every day not only survive but live and ENJOY to the fullest a life raising 4 beautiful little boys and being married to one wonderful husband along with coping with anxiety and depression. Thank you and please never ever stop writing!   —AMY
>
> I wish I could convey to you how much your daily messages mean to me. As I struggle with my inner hell, sometimes you are the only light in the day. Thank you again from the bottom of my heart.   —RACHEL

In 2010, Center Street Books published Therese's memoir, *Beyond Blue: Surviving Depression and Anxiety and Making the Most of Bad Genes.* Psychologist John Grohol, founder of PsychCentral.com, wrote: "Therese is a rare writer who can have you laughing one moment and crying the next. Her book *Beyond Blue* is a testament to the unwavering resiliency of the human spirit."

When she was on her author tour, many interviewers asked Therese: "You say, here, that Catholicism is the best religion for the mentally ill. You're joking, right?"

Therese would talk about her childhood. "When I was wrapped in anxiety, afraid to shut my eyes at night, nothing could console me more than reading Psalm 91. I used to sing the lyrics to 'Be Not Afraid' in the shower. While I know meditation has the power to change your brain and deliver calm, I still can't do anything but pray the rosary when my manic depressive noggin is juggling a dozen negative thoughts a minute. Everything is wasted on that brain but a group of Our Fathers and Hail Marys because when depression strikes I don't have the energy or the ability to come up with something original to say to the Creator or anyone else for that matter."

Then Therese talks about Mother Teresa, whom she met in Calcutta as a volunteer when she was twenty-two. "I respect her even more now," Therese says. "Her diaries allowed us a glimpse into her desolation and despair. To think she accomplished all she did while battling her own demons . . . well, that gives me reason to think that my neurotic brain doesn't mean the end of all good and charitable things either. Catholicism is the best religion for me not because of its security blankets for insecure people like me but because of its people—Mother Teresa, Thérèse of Lisieux, Henry Nouwen, Thomas Merton, and, of course, my husband and my friends—who help me through meltdowns and to get through one day at a time with sanity and peace."

And, of course, the miracle of weeping at Jesus' feet.

Therese Borchard, a recovering everything, *is* sun-shine. Few clouds pass over her light anymore, but when they do, she still glows and reaches out to those who are hurting in the dark. Henri Nouwen, the great spiritual writer of the twentieth century, wrote:

> Nobody escapes being wounded. We all are wounded people, whether physically, emotionally, mentally, or spiritually. The main question is not "How can we hide our wounds?" so we don't have to be embarrassed, but "How can we put our woundedness in the service of others?" When our wounds cease to be a source of shame, and become a source of healing, we have become wounded healers.

Therese Borchard stays Catholic because of role models like Nouwen. I stay Catholic because of friends like Therese.

Come and see: www.thereseborchard.com and *http://blog .beliefnet.com/beyondblue/* and *Beyond Blue* by Therese Borchard

John Smyth

33

God's Hands: John Smyth

*Let the little children come to me, and do not stop them; for
it is to such as these that the kingdom of heaven belongs.*
—MATTHEW 19:14, NRSV

The statue of Fr. John Smyth and "the flying child" stands
near the entrance of Maryville Academy, a home for
dependent children in Des Plaines, Illinois. It is larger
than life. John Smyth is larger than life. He is to Maryville
what Fr. Flanagan was to Boys Town, to children in our
time what St. John Bosco (1815–1888) was to his, and to
disadvantaged families from Chicago what Mother Teresa
was to those written off by society in Calcutta. This is not
an exaggeration. John Smyth has dedicated his life to seeing that no child gets left behind, even those who don't
have a chance, and thousands of them who are now successful adults will tell you that Michael Jordan's statue in
front of Chicago Stadium is an ornament compared to
John Smyth's at the City of Youth. Fr. Smyth stands for the
timeless truth that "No person stands so tall as the one
who stoops to help a child."

I was a priest at Maryville with John in the 1960s. We had known each other in the seminary but lived together at Maryville twenty-four hours a day with two other priests, two dozen Sisters of Providence, and six hundred boys and girls from kindergarten through high school who could have been stars in *Oliver!* or *West Side Story* on Broadway (disclosure: I put on those plays with the kids in the gym, the most satisfying creative experience I have ever had). John had been at Maryville for four years, and I was newly ordained. My forever memory of John is the day we welcomed an eight-year-old boy to his new home. The boy was anxious. John took the boy's hand into his. It was like a goldfish being cradled in a first baseman's glove. The boy looked up to John and exclaimed, "God's hands!"

Did I tell you that John is six-foot-six and was an All-American basketball star at Notre Dame and first-round draft pick of the St. Louis Hawks? He decided to become a priest instead, but to this day he is proud of the NCAA record he set that still stands: most personal fouls. "I couldn't run, couldn't jump, and couldn't shoot," he jokes, "but God gave me two good elbows, and I used them." If Fr. Smyth has a flaw, it's that he has a fervor to win that makes Michael Jordan's look like a low-grade fever. But even those who think his ego is too big for his collar will tell you this: all John has ever wanted to win for the past forty-nine years is a good life for his kids.

John Smyth became executive director of Maryville in 1970. When I was there, Maryville was an old Catholic movie with Fr. Bing Crosby and Sr. Ingrid Bergman and Our Gang with attitude. In 1968 the world turned upside down. Maryville was still a haven for children from poor or broken homes but was also welcoming children with new, more shattering experiences and special needs. John refused to refuse any child or teenager who had been refused elsewhere. "There's no such thing as a kid who can't be saved," was his refrain. John had also seen the future in 1966 and had hired social workers and a psychologist, but by 1970 Maryville had become a financial drain on the archdiocese, and the buildings, just like the crumbling school in *The Bells of St. Mary's,* were beyond repair. The cardinal could sell the hundred-acre property to real-estate developers for a fortune. What Fr. Smyth needed to accomplish to save Maryville from the wrecking ball and remain a home for children was nothing more than a miracle.

So he exceeded expectations.

With help from his friends at Notre Dame, John put Maryville in the black without a dime from the Archdiocese. John would even mow the fields himself so the kids could play ball. He introduced the Family Teaching Model, replacing the old three-story dorms with modern residential cottages where the children participated in managing their own homes. They took part in chores, menu planning, grocery shopping, and budgeting under the supervision of a live-in married couple and supported by a team of social workers and counselors. John held an annual chuckwagon fund-raiser on the grounds, and soon the number of Maryville volunteers soared into the hundreds. John was a magnet for those who wanted to help young people. Cubs and Bears and Blackhawks left their lairs to come and play with the kids; rock stars like Pete Townshend gave multiple concerts to raise money for satellite homes; philanthropists, politicians, and celebrities flocked to the City of Youth to "stoop down and lift up a child."

The spirit of the City of Youth in Des Plaines, Illinois, spread to Chicago like a New Testament breeze. Over the next two decades Fr. Smyth and his team would expand Maryville to more than eighteen inner-city sites, caring each year for more than sixteen thousand neglected, abused, and abandoned youth. These centers treat cocaine-addicted newborns; toddlers with complex medical needs; teenagers with mental illness and substance-abuse problems; teenage girls at odds with the law; victims of prostitution, child pornography, and sexual abuse; and children damaged by family violence, and include a state-of-the-art psychiatric hospital for children up to the age of twenty-one. These are fruits of an incredible life.

And there's more. Always devoted to the Blessed Mother, John built a shrine to Our Lady of Guadalupe on the grounds in 1988 at the request of Hispanic Catholics. It was just one of those things that John would say yes to and then do, but who could have known that before long, three thousand worshippers, mostly Latin American, would be attending Mass at the site every weekend? Each December 11 and 12, up to one hundred thousand Catholics make the pilgrimage to Des Plaines to celebrate her feast day. They come wrapped in winter coats, carrying babies and banners and roses to place at the foot of Mary's statue. For Fr. Smyth, the day of the statue's installation back in 1988 had been just another day.

John is seventy-six now, well past the mandatory retirement age for a parish priest. So what is he doing with his time? Watching 16mm films of his foul-filled glory days at Notre Dame? No way. John is now president of Notre Dame High School in Niles, Illinois. His vision is to produce a new generation of Catholic ethical leaders. Always relying on Mary, one of the first things John did was build a shrine to Our Lady of Lourdes at the entrance of the school, similar to the one at the University of Notre Dame—only three feet taller and three feet wider.

Never one to stand still, he also established the Standing Tall Charitable Foundation to provide assistance to homeless, underserved, and at-risk families. A *Sun-Times* reporter once observed that you might catch Fr. Smyth on a Chicagoland golf course a couple dozen times a year, but not golfing. "I hate golf. I don't golf. I stand there like an idiot and shake everybody's hands." Why does he do it? "To raise $1.4 million to send two hundred kids to college."

As you can imagine, Fr. Smyth has received many honors, including the prestigious Laetare Medal from Notre Dame. Established in 1883, the Laetare Medal has been worn only "by men and women whose genius has ennobled the arts and sciences, illustrated the ideals of the Church, and enriched the heritage of humanity." Other recipients include President John F. Kennedy, Cardinal Joseph Bernardin, Sr. Thea Bowman, Supreme Court Justice William J. Brennan, and Catholic Worker movement founder Dorothy Day.

But no honor can be greater than the gratitude of thousands of children who have been his life for five decades. When I was at Maryville, I often saw John race to his beat-up Ford late at night to drive to the city to help a family in trouble. Sure, all the priests did that from time to time, but John has been doing it for half a century— and still is! You could fall asleep counting the marriages, baptisms, and, yes, funerals John has performed at the request of Maryville alumni over the decades. They still see him, call him, and write him, and he does the same.

Stephanie Winter, who came to Maryville as a little girl in 1968, heard I was writing this book, and she e-mailed me.

"Mike," she wrote, "I don't think being Catholic is about the rituals or things like that. For me being Catholic is about the hand extended to you, letting you know that you are not now or ever will be alone. That hand in my life happened over forty years ago. It was the hand of Father John Smyth who for years I have affectionately referred to as 'Father Dad.' He is what being Catholic is to me. The unexpected phone call in my darkest moments. The comfort in his voice, the reassurance that things will be better. 'Have faith and always remain hopeful, a little humble, and always keep a smile on your face.' Let me share with you a thank-you I wrote to him only a few months ago in hopes that this great big Catholic man would have at least a small idea of how much I appreciated him through the years. These are my own words of thanks, not a card's, to Fr. Smyth:

From me to you. For your kindness, your thoughtful caring heart. For always being my hero, my comfort, my peace of mind. You lift my spirit, renew and strengthen my faith. You are a reoccurring [sic] hope in a world gone mad. Like that first ray of sunshine that breaks through after a week of rain and bone-chilling cold, you are there shining bright, a shoulder to lean on. An inspiration of hope for a better tomorrow. For these gifts and so much more I thank you. With all the love and appreciation any child could have for their Dad, I thank you.   —STEPHANIE

Why stay Catholic when some priests in the church have done the unspeakable?

The answer is in God's Hands.

Come and see: standingtallfoundation.org and maryvilleacademy.org

Walter Burghardt

34

God's Voice: Walter Burghardt

Here is my servant whom I have chosen, the one I love,
in whom I delight; I will put my Spirit on him, and
he will proclaim justice to the nations.
—MATTHEW 12:18, NIV

Walter called me a few days before his death. "Hello?" he said. "Who is it?"

I said what I said every time I'd pick up the phone and hear his warm baritone voice. "Walter, how good to hear your voice!"

This time there was a pause, and Walter asked again, "Who is this?"

"It's Mike."

"How good to hear from you!" he said. "Thank you for calling me!"

I knew something was up.

But it was the same dear Walter. He asked about Vickie, as he always did. "She's right here," I said. "She wants to say hello."

"Hello, Vickie," he said. "I am praying for you at Mass every day." And he was, for four years, since the day we received the diagnosis of Alzheimer's.

"It means everything to me," she said.

That was the last we heard from Walter, but Vickie and I will remember his voice forever. It was deep and rich and good and kind—just as God's voice must be.

Walter Burghardt, SJ (1914–2008), was a spiritual giant who spoke softly and stooped toward you so he could hear *your* voice. He was the greatest Catholic preacher of the twentieth century and also its greatest listener. His craggy face was a map of a life well traveled down roads of joy and up rivers of suffering. In his eyes, people saw oases of compassion and peace. A Jesuit for seventy-seven years, he taught at Woodstock College, Catholic University, Union Theological Seminary, and Princeton Theological Seminary. He was the author of three hundred seminal articles, and among his twenty-five books are fifteen collections of his sermons. He also published an autobiography, *Long Have I Loved You*, which won first prize from the Catholic Press Association, also scholarly books on church history and social justice. Fr. Burghardt's twenty-one honorary degrees testify to the respect he earned among academics and educators throughout the world.

When Walter was nearing age eighty, he retired as editor-in-chief of the journal *Theological Studies*. He went to his friend Jim Connor and asked, "Now what do I do?" Fr. Connor recalls how they talked long into the night. "First," we concluded, "whatever he did should have something to do with preaching. That was Walter's gift. Second, it ought to have something to do with the contemporary mission of the Society of Jesus, namely, serving faith by promoting justice. Finally, its influence should be as widespread as possible."

Connor's idea ignited a fire in Walter's imagination. "Think about this," Walter said to Jim. "Every Sunday in the United States thousands of preachers are speaking to millions of people in the pews. Imagine the impact for the good of society if these homilies inspired all those people to engage serious issues of social justice and to work to heal them!"

In 1991, Father Burghardt, with arthritic knees and failing eyesight, took off on a global adventure called "Preaching the Just Word." He led more than 125 intensive, five-day retreats for thousands of priests and deacons in every part of the world. His goal was to inspire them to preach social justice from the pulpit. "He had this wonderful way with words, and he really had something to say," said Fr. Ray Kemp, a former Washington parish priest who accompanied Fr. Burghardt on most of the retreats. "He would make the prophets people you could understand. He believed the prophetic voice was speaking to real human need."

"Just imagine the miles that Walter logged," recalls Father Connor, "and all of this while in his eighties and nineties, and also while he was gradually losing his sight because of wet macular degeneration."

Later Walter wrote a book inspired by his years on the road with "Preaching the Just Word." It is *Justice: A Global*

Adventure, the second book of his that I had the privilege of editing and publishing. I was so happy when he said it was his favorite.

The first book we worked on was his memoir, *Long Have I Loved You*, and later his last book, *Short Sermons for Preachers on the Run*, published shortly after his death. Walter was housebound in his nineties and we became BPFs, best phone friends. We talked about books and the church and God and life. Walter was always more interested in my thoughts or endeavors than he was in his own. Only the great ones are like that.

Everyone at Orbis Books loved to receive phone calls from Fr. Burghardt. They knew "God's voice" right away and always told others how wonderful he was to work with, how grateful he was for the smallest favors, and how sweet he was. We sent Walter laminated plaques of his covers, as we do all authors. He hung them on his wall as if they had been designed by Michelangelo, and he showed them to everyone. It wasn't pride but simple gratitude for people who loved him enough to make that small gesture.

Only the *really* great ones are like that.

When Walter went nearly blind during the last five years of his life, he worked with his friend Kathy Waldron in continuing to write. His creativity was a fountain of youth that nothing could stop. Close to sightless, he was thrilled to write an article on vision for a medical journal. Kathy was an angel who visited Walter at Manresa Hall during his illnesses, and she became his bridge to the wider world. Walter told me about a new book of "short sermons for preachers on the run" that he was writing with Kathy's help. He asked me to be sure to mention her somewhere in the book because he couldn't do it without her.

"Of course, Walter," I said. "We can do anything you want. And, after all, that would only be justice."

"Justice . . ." I could hear the smile in his voice. "Yes," he said, "if I die then, make sure Kathy finishes it, and then you publish it. I think priests might find it helpful."

Only the greatest ones are like that.

I miss God's voice.

Let's listen to it right now—the voice of Fr. Burghardt on staying Catholic. It's the sweetest voice you will hear in this book.

I have seen more Catholic corruption than you have read of. I have tasted it. I have been reasonably corrupt myself. And yet I [take] joy in this Church—this living, pulsing, sinning people of God, love it with a crucifying passion. Why? For all the Catholic hate, I experience here a community of *love*. For all the institutional idiocy, I find here a tradition of *reason*. For all the individual repressions, I breathe here an air of *freedom*. For all the fear of sex, I discover here the redemption of the *body*. In an age so inhuman, I touch here the tears of *compassion*. In a world so grim and humorless, I share here rich *joy* and *laughter*. In the midst of death, I hear an incomparable stress on *life*. For all the apparent absence of God, I sense here the real presence of *Christ!*   —*TELL THE NEXT GENERATION*

Come and see: http://woodstock.georgetown.edu/programs/ Preaching-the-Just-Word.html and *Justice: A Global Adventure* and *Long Have I Loved You: A Theologian Reflects on His Church* by Walter Burghardt

Dorothy Day

35

Godmother: Dorothy Day

Love is the measure by which we will be judged.
—Dorothy Day, after John of the Cross

The next canonized American saint will be an unwed mother from Brooklyn.

Dorothy Day (1897–1980) was also an anarchist, activist, and pacifist who was arrested more times than the Chicago Seven, shot at by the KKK, and investigated by J. Edgar Hoover. As a young woman she had several love affairs, at least one abortion, and an attempted suicide. At her death, historian David O'Brien called her "the most influential, interesting, and significant figure in the history of American Catholicism."

What is amazing about Dorothy Day is not that so few Catholics know anything about her but that so many who do are young adults who were barely alive when she died in 1980. Therese Borchard discovered Dorothy when she was studying religion at St. Mary's College. "What attracted me to Dorothy Day is that she became holy despite so much baggage in her past, or maybe that she was able to transform all that baggage into holiness."

Dorothy's appeal is that she was a real woman—passionate, attractive, emotional, and tough—who blessed those around her by being herself. She once said, "Women think with their whole bodies and they see things as a whole more than men do." Dorothy was no plaster saint. She was the real thing.

So how did a child whose parents never went to church or even said the word *God* grow up to be an exemplar of Catholic social teaching in the twentieth century?

When Dorothy was a girl, her family moved from a brownstone in Brooklyn Heights with a view of Manhattan to a Victorian with a garden in Oakland to a cold-water flat over a tavern in Chicago. Her father, a sportswriter, had lost his job when the San Francisco earthquake demolished the paper's printing plant in 1906. The Depression came early to the Day family.

Dorothy found a Bible in the attic and began to read it. "I remember nothing that I read, just the sense of holiness in holding the book in my hands." She began to read the lives of the saints. A neighbor lady taught her to pray. She walked the cobbled streets of Chicago and saw bony horses pulling wagons of ice, coalmen with dirty faces shoveling coal through basement transoms, women lugging babies under each arm like shopping bags, with other kids circling around them, and she considered the human condition. Dorothy saw herself in each of them. She began to know: all of us are somehow mysteriously one.

Dorothy's faith in God grew, but as a teenager she often wondered where God was in the slums and factories and mean streets, where people hungered and labored and scratched to make a living. She knew about the saints and dreamt about giving her life for the poor, the sick, and the dying. But another question burned in her mind: "Why was so much done in remedying the evil instead of avoiding it in the first place?" Dorothy devoured novels with a social conscience: books by Jack London and Upton Sinclair, Charles Dickens and Victor Hugo, Tolstoy and Dostoevsky. She began to write, and her passion for words matched her compassion for the downtrodden:

> Disabled men, men without arms and legs, blind, con-sumptive, exhausted men with all the manhood drained from them by industrialism; farmers gaunt and harried with debt; mothers weighted down with children at their skirts, in their arms, in their wombs, and the children ailing, rickety, toothless—all this long procession of desperate people called to me. Where were the saints to try to change the social order, not just to minister to the slaves but to do away with slavery?

Dorothy's passion took her to the Lower East Side of New York when she was nineteen. She lived a bohemian life in Greenwich Village, partied with young writers such as Hart Crane and Eugene O'Neill, protested for workers' and women's rights, even hung around with blowhards who talked like terrorists. She worked as a journalist for socially conscious magazines and often took the night shift at Kings County Hospital where she changed bedpans, made beds, and cleaned wounds. She read *The Imitation of Christ* so many times the pages wrinkled like old leaves. And when her daughter, Tamar, was born in 1926, Dorothy Day was born again. "No human creature could receive or contain so vast a flood of love and joy as I often felt after the birth of my child. With this came the need to worship, to adore."

Dorothy had Tamar baptized in the Catholic Church. "I did not want my child to flounder as I had often floundered," she wrote. "I wanted to believe, and I wanted my child to believe, and if belonging to a Church would give her so inestimable a grace as faith in God, and the companionable love of the Saints, then the thing to do was to have her baptized a Catholic." Dorothy herself received baptism at Our Lady Help of Christians parish on Staten Island just one year later.

Everything came together in Dorothy's life—her love for Tamar, the poor, the church—when she met Peter Maurin in 1932. He was a Catholic visionary who saw the need of a newspaper to proclaim the social message of the gospel, houses of hospitality to practice the corporal works of mercy, and farming communes where "workers could become scholars and scholars could become workers." Five months later on a sunny corner in Union Square, editor Dorothy Day was hawking her first issue of *The Catholic Worker* for a penny per copy. The first printing of 2,500 copies sold out the same day. In a few months it was 25,000 copies, and three years later, 150,000 copies.

Dorothy wrote an editorial on the first page of the first issue that made William Randolph Hearst's statement of purpose in his first *San Francisco Examiner* look like a limerick. She wrote that *The Catholic Worker* stood for, next to, and behind anyone who labored—physically, mentally, spiritually—but especially "those who are huddling in shelters trying to escape the rain, for those who are walking the streets in all but futile search for work, for those who think that there is no hope for the future, no recognition for their plight." The paper's dream was "a new society within the shell of the old, a society in which it will be easier to be good."

The Catholic Worker was Catholic to its core. It put forth the social teachings of the church as an antidote to communism, which was a flashing neon sign during those dark days of the Depression. It proclaimed Catholicism's best-kept secret: the church has a social program, too, and is interested not only in your spiritual welfare but also your material well-being. Dorothy Day's radical leanings now leaned completely on the Sermon on the Mount.

Out of *The Catholic Worker* rose the Catholic Worker movement. Run-down tenements in inner cities became houses of hospitality where volunteers offered shelter, clothing, food, and friendship to the poor. Today more than 180 Catholic Worker communities practice hospitality for the homeless, live lives of poverty and prayer, and promote nonviolence and human rights. Its alumni are editors and publishers, union leaders and university professors, monks and nuns and married couples. The paper still sells for only a penny per copy.

Dorothy once wrote, "What we do is very little, but it's like the little boy with a few loaves and fishes. Christ took that little and increased it. He will do the rest."

Dorothy Day oversaw *The Catholic Worker* for almost fifty years. She gave birth not only to Tamar but to several generations of peacemakers. She was a grandmother to nine children and the godmother to a Catholic lay movement that gave birth to the Catholic Peace Fellowship, Pax Christi, the witnesses for peace of those such as the Berrigan brothers, and the groundbreaking U.S. Bishop's pastoral letter *The Challenge of Peace*.

Through all that time, working in an office the size of a jail cell and going to prison on behalf of the voiceless, she was first and foremost a woman whose heart was as big as a cathedral. Dorothy loved to wander through the asphalt jungle of Manhattan just as she did the mean streets of Chicago.

Early one morning on the steps of Precious Blood Church, a woman with cancer on the face was begging (beggars are allowed only in the slums) and when I gave her money (no sacrifice on my part but merely passing on alms which someone had given me) she tried to kiss my hand. The only thing I could do was kiss her dirty old face with the gaping hole in it where an eye and a nose had been. It sounds like a heroic deed but it was not. One gets used to ugliness so quickly. What we avert our eyes from one day is easily borne the next when we have learned a little more about love. Nurses know that, and so do mothers.

Dorothy Day was a woman, a mother, a lover, a friend, a poet, and a prophet. She was just like us.

She made the most of what she was. Near the end of her life *Newsweek, Life,* and *Time* praised her, citing her in a cover story about "Living Saints." "Please don't call me a saint," Dorothy would tell people. "I don't want to be dismissed so easily."

An admirer once approached an aged Dorothy and asked her, "Miss Day, do you have visions?" Her response: "Oh, shit!"

Dorothy Day passed away in 1980 at age eighty-three.

In 2000 Cardinal John O'Connor, with support from the U.S. Conference of Catholic Bishops and the enthusiasm of laity who would never dismiss her, began the canonization process of Dorothy Day. She was given the title Servant of God. Today Archbishop Timothy Dolan continues the process to declare Dorothy a saint—no matter how much she protests in heaven.

Come and see: dorothydayguild.org and catholicworker.org and *Love Is the Measure: A Biography of Dorothy Day* by Jim Forest and *Dorothy Day: Selected Writings,* edited by Robert Ellsberg

Raymond Lucker

36

The Bishop: Raymond Lucker

*How God loves us! With an everlasting love, a merciful
love that is faithful and never changes even though we
forget him, even if we reject him, even if we sin against him.
The good news that Jesus came to bring us is this: God
loves me. He doesn't love me only when I am good or
because I am good. He just loves me. He made me.
He continues to care for me. He sent his Son to prove it.
Even when I sin? Yes!*

—RAYMOND A. LUCKER

"Ray Lucker can afford to be an outspoken bishop," said
the insiders. "He isn't going anywhere."

That's just the way the bishop of New Ulm,
Minnesota, liked it. Raymond A. Lucker (1927–2001)
wasn't interested in climbing a ladder unless it was to
fix a roof. He was born in St. Paul, one of six children
of Alphonse Lucker, a railroad worker, and Josephine
Schiltgen, a farmer's daughter. The kitchen table was
the heart of their working-class home. The vast land
outside the city limits promised anything was possible.

To Ray Lucker, Minnesota was heaven. He didn't need to go anywhere else.

When Ray Lucker became bishop of New Ulm in 1976, he knew the lay of the land better than Henry Hudson did New Jersey in 1609. The diocese of New Ulm is larger than the entire state of New Jersey, but Jersey has six dioceses and twelve bishops, New Ulm only one. So the first thing the new bishop did was to drive to every one of his eighty parishes throughout the ten thousand square miles of farms, lakes, and prairies. The diocese had fewer than eighty priests, many of them retired, serving eighty thousand Catholics and thousands of migrant workers who came each year to harvest crops. Bishop Lucker encouraged his priests, kept in touch with them, and was the first bishop in the United States to support his priests with pastoral administrators so they could focus on being priests. He invited every pastor and their lay leaders to regional assemblies where they could meet other priests and laity from the diocese and share their vision of church with one another.

"I believe in the parish," Bishop Lucker told them. "You are the Church in miniature. You are a community of people united by a bond of divine grace—a fellowship in the Spirit." Bishop Lucker had five priorities for the diocese: strengthening of parish life, spiritual renewal, Catholic education, rural life, and the diocese's mission in Guatemala. Lucker often visited the parish of San Lucas Toliman in Guatemala, endeavoring to be a mirror of grace reflecting God's love to the Mayans and, in turn, bringing back to Minnesotans images of their goodness. He would often tell his Minnesota Catholics how proud he was of them for making a commitment to the poor:

> San Lucas is our parish just as truly as any other parish in our fifteen-county area. It is our largest parish, serving half as many people as there are in our diocese. It is our poorest parish because the income they can expect from the sacrifices of their poor is only about $8,000 a year. It is our richest parish because through the work of their people and the support of our people it carries on a program of help and self-improvement that no other parish in our diocese even needs. It is a big program because the needs are big. There is no part that can be eliminated without putting little children out on the street, sending the sick to lie uncared for on the bare dirt, or allowing the next generation to grow up uneducated.

Bishop Lucker related to every Catholic in his diocese as if they were family members, which he knew they were. He had a special bond with the migrant workers who came each summer and with the Native Americans who had lived there long before the immigrants from Germany and Sweden made Minnesota their home. When he learned that some Mexican-American migrant workers were being scalded with obscenities and racial slurs and had no choice but to live in subhuman conditions, Bishop Lucker made it clear to everyone in the diocese how much it pained him and how it wounds everyone when "such beautiful, gentle people are so harshly treated." He urged his parishes to reach out to them and his diocesan office to institute programs to help them. At Bishop Lucker's funeral in 2001, the wife of a leader of the Dakota tribe placed in his coffin a beaded medallion, symbolizing his friendship with Native Americans. "He was one of the few priests that really made us comfortable here in New Ulm," she said. "He accomplished a great deal because, up to then, we weren't really accepted."

Bishop Lucker was the first American bishop to advocate women's rights in the church. He wrote to his flock: "I am interested in listening to the experiences of the daily lives of women in church and society." He hosted open dialogues with women on the role of women in the church. He advocated the ordination of women and married men at the U.S. Conference of Catholic Bishops' annual meetings. Not a few of his fellow bishops asked him to back off. That didn't deter him. He wasn't going anywhere.

Bishop Lucker could have lived a comfortable life in a bishop's manse in New Ulm. He chose instead to live in a community at the old pastoral center. "I can say that one of the greatest blessings of my life is that I live with a faith-filled, praying, caring community. There are nine of us: four other priests, three sisters, and a laywoman who prepares the evening meal. We live together, eat together, pray together, share together, and yes, cry together. We tend the garden, freeze and can vegetables, do most of the laundry, prepare meals, decorate, make small repairs, do the shopping, and tend to the other details of the household. In all of this we find Jesus, who is already here and who is the center of our community."

Bishop Lucker loved gardening. His mother had been a farm girl. "Gardening is a meditation," he wrote. "It teaches me how precious life is." He liked to cook for others when he had time. Long before Paul Newman invented salad dressing, Ray Lucker was creating his own soup and jelly. "Lucker's is better than Smucker's!" he boasted. When driving back from parish visits, he'd stop on the sides of roads and gather mushrooms for his unique brew of soup, hot and salty, which he delighted in seeing others enjoy.

The bishop's visits to parishes often meant driving four hours each way. But his visit was never a "rush in, say Mass, have breakfast, and get back in the limo" kind of thing. First of all, he never had a limo; he drove his own car. And he told his people what the visits were all about:

> One of the best things I do all year is conduct official visitations of our parishes. [Each visit] takes a whole weekend. I visit the Catholic school, if there is one; I meet with teachers and catechists. I spend time listening to and supporting the parish staff; I speak with the parish council, committees, boards and organizations; I visit the shut-ins and anoint the sick; I participate in and speak at the parish liturgies; and I administer the sacrament of Confirmation. A heavy weekend, it usually leaves me exhausted. It also gives me a lift as I see and experience the wonderful things that God is doing among his people and the various ways that they are responding to his gifts.

I first met this unpretentious man in 1990. He was receiving an award from the National Catholic Education Association. Did I not tell you that Raymond Lucker was not only a straightforward, down-to-earth Minnesotan but also one of the pioneering Catholic educators of the twentieth century?

The young Fr. Lucker earned a doctorate of sacred theology and a PhD in education. He studied in Rome during the Second Vatican Council. The open windows of the Council gave the open-minded priest a vision of church that was much like Minnesota: a place where you could see forever in all directions. He returned home and soon became superintendent of schools for the archdiocese of St. Paul and Minneapolis. Fr. Lucker was so successful in advancing Catholic education that he was tapped to become director of the Department of Christian Formation of the U.S. Catholic Conference when he was forty-two, and he became a prime mover in the nationwide development of the Confraternity of Christian Doctrine. During his life he would be honored by numerous organizations, including the Catholic Theological Society. Pax Christi gave him its highest honor, the Ambassador of Peace Award, two years before his death.

In 1990 I shared with Bishop Lucker an idea for a catechism that would represent Vatican II's definition of church as "the people of God." Its editors and writers would include a bishop, priests, religious, and laypeople, and would consist of theologians and people in the pews. The book would be the first of its kind—a popular catechism *for* the people of God *by* the people of God. "Would you like to play with me on this?" I asked him. Five years later *The People's Catechism* was published with Raymond A. Lucker as its lead editor.

In 2000, Bishop Lucker was diagnosed with malignant melanoma. He retired as bishop of New Ulm on November 17, 2000, having served for twenty-five years. Everyone in New Ulm and millions of other Catholics who knew about him grieved. While he lay dying at Our Lady of Good Counsel Home in St. Paul, Bishop Lucker told friends, "I am just sitting here and letting Jesus love me."

Do some bishops in the church bother you? Me, too. I stay Catholic because I knew Ray Lucker, and because I know there are other bishops who share his values. We just don't read about them in the papers.

As for Bishop Lucker, he went somewhere all right. He went to the place he never left: heaven.

Come and see: dnu.org/news/091901news.html and *The People's Catechism: Catholic Faith for Adults,* edited by Raymond Lucker, Patrick Brennan, and Michael Leach

Toni Bosco with son Peter two years before his death

37

Model of Forgiveness: Antoinette Bosco

*Love your enemies and pray for those who hurt you, that
you may be children of your loving Father in heaven. God's
sun shines on the good and the bad, and his rain falls on
the righteous and the unrighteous.*
—MATTHEW 5:44–45

Amazon.com lists 160,510 books on the topic of forgiveness. That's 31,629 more than on sexuality. What does that tell us about the human heart and what it hungers for most?

As an editor and publisher, I ask authors to write on topics that interest me deeply. Over the years I've asked more authors to write on the topic of forgiveness than on any other. That's because I want to get it right in my own life. Nothing is more important. Who of us doesn't desire the freedom that comes when we let go of resentments that sear our souls, or the joy that makes our hearts soar when we ourselves experience forgiveness?

The two best books on forgiveness I've ever published are both by Antoinette (Toni) Bosco. Toni is a woman who knows what she's talking about. She lost one son to suicide and another son and his wife to the hands of a cold-blooded killer. Can you imagine how she felt toward God, toward herself, and toward the murderer of her child? Toni's life since has been a dramatic journey to radical forgiveness and inner peace.

When her youngest son, Peter, the joy of her life, killed himself at age twenty-seven, Toni, a single mother, did not have much time to grieve. She had to help her other six children, who adored Peter, get through their grief. Peter had first suffered a nervous breakdown when he was seventeen. With the help of family and professionals, he slowly recovered and went on to write three books, one of them on World War I and another on the War of 1812. Peter hated war, and when the Gulf War started, he felt he could no longer live in this kind of world. His suicide note said, "Be happy for your son. . . . My pain is gone."

Toni was still mourning Peter's death when two years later the phone rang in the middle of the night. It was a Montana sheriff, two thousand miles away from the Bosco home in Connecticut.

"Are you Antoinette Bosco?" he asked.

"Yes," she answered.

"Do you have a son John Bosco?"

"What's wrong? What happened?"

"I'm sorry to have to tell you this, but we have a crime scene here. He and his wife are dead."

Toni couldn't speak.

When she climbed up the stairs of the Montana home and entered the blood-soaked bedroom, Toni wanted to kill the killer with her bare hands. She wanted him dead.

She would break into a sweat every time she saw in her mind's eye the eighteen-year-old with the unlikely name of Shadow Clark crawling through the basement window into her children's home, sneaking up the stairs to the bedroom where they slept, and then, afraid they would awaken, shooting them to death with a semiautomatic gun.

In time, in spite of my grieving, which will always be a permanent part of my life, I knew I had to reclaim my soul, but how? I had to struggle long and hard with whether forgiveness made sense, whether it was even possible. My children helped me as we struggled together with this horror. We had always been opposed to the death penalty, and began to grasp again that the state is no more justified in taking a life than an individual. Our healing began when we wrote to the judge, asking that Shadow Clark not be executed. I could say he must be punished for life, but I could not say, kill this killer.

I learned to see that the minute we say "no" to forgiveness we are gouging Christ out of our life, and from that resulting emptiness of soul we have nothing left to give to anybody else.

To forgive is just what the word itself says—to offer a gift before it's been earned or even deserved. It doesn't mean giving in; it means letting go. If we don't forgive, we stay emotionally handcuffed to the person—or the nation—that hurt us. And if we're handcuffed, we are not free, never at peace, never able to do God's work. Forgiveness is a boomerang—the gift we send out is what we're going to get back. This is how God treats us. When we forgive, we act as God does.

Toni realized it was foolishness to think that her pain would end by making someone else feel pain. She knew that revenge, too, was a boomerang. Her whole life as a Catholic taught her to rely on the teachings of Jesus to get through suffering. She knew that Jesus' entire life was about forgiveness. "Now again he was helping me take the actions that would bring healing. Each step in my life was clearly marked with directions : *"Forgive!* Forgive your troubled Peter, forgive the young killer of your John and Nancy, forgive yourself."

Without asking for it, Toni soon became a national advocate against capital punishment. She has been invited to speak against the death penalty at high schools and colleges, in parishes and in prisons. The U.S. Conference of Catholic Bishops asked her to speak to them on forgiveness. The U.S. Senate asked her to submit testimony at a special hearing on the death penalty.

"When we are crushed like grapes," wrote Henri Nouwen, "we cannot think of the wine we will become."

Toni Bosco is vintage Catholicism.

She speaks to *us* in *Radical Forgiveness:*

Few people, thank God, have to deal with forgiving someone who murdered a loved one, or a beloved child who is defeated in life and ends his or her pain by killing themselves. But all of us must deal on a regular basis with thoughts about people we feel have hurt us, abandoned us, spoken badly about us, hurt our feelings, damaged our reputations, manipulated, provoked, or just plain annoyed us. They can be parents, relatives, friends, bosses, employees, or strangers.

But it is not these people we need to forgive so much as our thoughts about them, the angry, unforgiving thoughts that gnaw at our consciousness, burn us, haunt us, won't let us go, because we can't let *them* go. I have learned that radical forgiveness, asked for and given, seventy times seven times is the only way out of that prison.

A prize-winning journalist, Toni has written more than two hundred magazine articles, thousands of newspaper stories, and ten books, but was awarded the Christopher Award, the Catholic Press Award, and the Pax Christi Award for two of her books on forgiveness: *The Pummeled Heart* and *Choosing Mercy: A Mother of Murder Victims Pleads to End the Death Penalty.* Yes, there are 160,510 books on forgiveness, and many of them are extraordinary, but Toni Bosco, you can be sure, knows what she is talking about. Her example enables the rest of us to deal with the "little murders"—gossip, backstabbing, envy, resentment—that torture each of us.

Many Catholics feel resentment toward God or the church. No one can blame them. But it may help for all of us to know that Catholicism, spiritually understood, was a source of healing for Toni Bosco, a woman who has suffered greatly and who is one of the most together people you could ever know. "Buoyed by the grace of God," she says, "I found my answer. It is not to want more death. It is to celebrate *life*" (John 10:10).

Come and see: antoinettebosco.com and *The Pummeled Heart* and *Choosing Mercy: A Mother of Murder Victims Pleads to End the Death Penalty* and *Radical Forgiveness* by Antoinette Bosco

Marybeth Christie Redmond

38

A Catholic Family Value:
Marybeth Christie Redmond

*You don't choose your family. They are God's gift
to you, as you are to them.*
—DESMOND TUTU

The first time I saw Marybeth Christie was on television late at night. She was standing in the middle of railroad tracks with a microphone in her hand, reporting the death of a mother and her three children on our local news station. The mother had been fleeing an abusive husband and was leading her kids to a homeless shelter in the next town under dark of night when a train smashed into them, tossing their bodies like rag dolls to both sides of the tracks. Marybeth was visibly shaken but reported the news professionally. I recalled Walter Cronkite announcing the death of John F. Kennedy with his emotions stuck in his throat. I thought, this beautiful young woman cannot hide her compassion. She ought to be on network TV.

The second time was a year later, when Marybeth entered my office at Orbis Books with the kind of smile that lasts only seconds but you remember forever. "Hi, I'm Marybeth Christie, the new director of media relations for Maryknoll?" She said it like a question, so I answered, "Yes, I saw you on television."

Maryknoll—the Catholic Foreign Mission Society of America—is the parent of Orbis Books. I was Orbis's publisher. Marybeth would join me on the Maryknoll management team. She brought a glow to our meetings that even a killjoy couldn't snuff out. You know how it is when a negative voice smothers enthusiasm in a room? Marybeth was a salve for squeaky wheels. It wasn't network TV, but she spread the good news of Maryknoll's work with the poor of the world better than anyone ever had done before.

Marybeth Christie left a promising career in television to broadcast God.

Ten years later she met and married her soulmate, Mark Redmond, gained the cleverest of teenage stepsons, and birthed a beautiful baby boy at age forty. Life was as good as it gets, but it never stays that way, does it? Mark, a kindred spirit, was offered a perfect job in Burlington, Vermont, as director of Spectrum Youth and Family Services. After discussing the pros and cons, the new family chose to go on a Vermont adventure. They packed up, said their good-byes, and moved to the green mountains. Marybeth loved being a wife and mom, but when Liam went to school, she wondered what else to do with the talents God had given her. She had always used her talents for good, but the only useful work she could find in Vermont was volunteering part-time to teach writing in a woman's prison. She was in her midforties. What to do with the rest of her life?

Marybeth went back to an excerpt from Rainer Maria Rilke's *Letters to a Young Poet*, which she had read hundreds of times since first learning it from Fr. John Dunne in a senior-year theology class at the University of Notre Dame:

> Be patient toward all that is unsolved in your heart and try to love the questions themselves like locked rooms and like books that are written in a very foreign tongue. Do not seek the answers, which cannot be given you because you would not be able to live them. And the point is, to live everything. Live the questions now. Perhaps you will then gradually, without noticing it, live along some distant day into the answer.

She prayed to God with an open heart. All she wanted was direction and clarity. And what she got—living the question, living everything—was to live into an answer that would blow the socks off film critic Roger Ebert if her life were a movie. He would surely write: "I love all the characters in this inspiring family film, but surely it is contrived. Do all the themes of a life ever come together as beautifully as this?"

Surely, but only when looking backwards.

So, since life *is* a movie, let's have a flashback.

Catholicism ran through the Christie family of Brightwaters, Long Island, like gold through a mountain. Marybeth's father, Bill, had once considered becoming a Maryknoll missionary. As a girl, Marybeth was an avid reader of *Share*, a Maryknoll magazine for children that told stories of people around the world who didn't have her advantages but lived their faith in joy. She stored them in a box, stacked by month, and kept them under her bed for years.

Bill, a former marine, worked hard at being a good husband and father and did equally well as a financial planner. When Marybeth was seven, he was able to buy a second house in Vermont for the family to take holidays. It was close to the Benedictine Monks of Weston Priory, where the family went to Mass. Marybeth loved the soothing melody of their chant, and most of all the monks' charity. They took in a refugee family from Guatemala and spoke of modern heroes like Archbishop Oscar Romero and the four American churchwomen martyred during the civil war in El Salvador. Marybeth knew all of the monks by name. They were like family.

Marybeth's mother, Maryann, the oldest of seven McNamaras, nurtured the five little Christies with love and affection and found time to bring communion to the sick, work in a hospitality center for the homeless, and visit nursing homes. Today she volunteers and fund-raises for a soup kitchen. When Marybeth was in high school, Maryann gave her Dorothy Day's autobiograpy, *The Long Loneliness*, and encouraged her to be true to herself and to God.

When she graduated from the University of Notre Dame in 1985, Marybeth landed a job as a TV reporter at the NBC affiliate in South Bend. One of her first on-air stories was reporting the opening of a Dismas House in 1986. Dismas House provides transitional housing for former prisoners in a family-like environment where healthy community values are nurtured, helping them return to productive lives. Its mission struck Marybeth as somehow being at the core of Catholic family values. She was Christiane Amanpour with a Dorothy Day consciousness.

When she married Mark Redmond, her Catholic concept of family expanded further to include a convicted murderer whom Mark visited in prison. She joined Mark in his visits and would soon bring their newborn son to meet Norberto, navigating the metal detectors with Liam cradled in her arms.

> Mark, Norberto, and I chatted in the visiting room amongst a diverse sea of humanity, guard radios blaring, people talking loudly, while Liam napped in my lap. I thought of the company that Jesus Christ sought out in his day—thieves, killers, the mentally ill and poor. I was surrounded by them all, and oddly enough, I felt utterly at peace, exactly where I needed to be, fully on-purpose. Afterwards, Norberto penned us a short note saying how moved he had been to see an infant. He hadn't witnessed innocence and vulnerability so close-up in a long time. This particular visit cemented a kind of extended family connection. In so many words, I could tell he appreciated my brave gesture, bringing my most sacred creation in a place filled with so many broken lives and violent pasts.

Birthday cards, phone calls, and visits to Norberto became part of their family life. Mark and Marybeth helped him receive a college education "on the inside." Liam's four-year-old prayers during nightly meals became, "Jesus, please give Norberto a good life."

"As the years progressed," Marybeth recalls, "it became apparent that this unique relationship was profoundly transforming my definition of family. Friends would inquire about Norberto's art and academics as if he were one of my own children. I had always resonated with biblical stories of Christ crossing the borders of his day, be they 'lines in the sand' involving sinners, or women, or diverse peoples. Our Lord specifically zeroed in on the outcasts, gazing beyond their human frailties and calling forth divineness. He also granted them full access to his loving being. This powerful combination resulted in instantaneous healing for so many. I believe Christ was transformed by these encounters too, being fully human. Herein lies an authentic, expansive blueprint of Catholic family, in my view, beyond biology, history, or geography. It's the value I hold most dear about the Catholic Church, and it's why I'm still under the tent."

Gradually, just as Rilke promised, Marybeth lived into the answer that was always there. By living the questions, living everything, and not asking God for anything but clarity, all the themes of her life came into place.

She cofounded a writing program with incarcerated women at Northwest State Correctional Facility in Swanton, Vermont.

Burlington Dismas House asked her to serve on its board in 2009.

In 2010, Dismas of Vermont appointed Marybeth its executive director. She succeeded Rita Whalen McCaffrey who founded the Dismas program in the state the same year that Marybeth covered the opening of Michiana Dismas House in South Bend!

At the farewell party and handing over of the torch to Marybeth, the monks of the Weston Priory came and sang. The seven-year-old Marybeth didn't know it at the time, but the monks had contributed some of their meager funds to its opening and continue now. The event was covered, of course, by a young reporter.

To Marybeth, it's all in the family. "It's the value I hold most dear."

Come and see: dismasofvermont.org and maryknoll.org

Vickie Leach

39

The Color of Gratitude: Vickie Leach

If the only prayer you ever say in your entire life is
"Thank You," that will be enough.
—MEISTER ECKHART

It was 1968, the year Kennedy and King were killed, the year of burning cities and the Chicago convention. Anything was possible. Even love.

I was twenty-eight, and a Catholic priest. I wanted to help other people and make them happy. As a seminarian I dreamt of burning myself out for Christ before I was forty, just like Don Bosco, my favorite saint. When I started to do that, I had second thoughts. I had thought I could love everybody and make things right for everyone but was learning the hard way that I couldn't really change anything. I began to wonder what it would be like to love just one person with all my heart and have a family and do just that one thing right.

I had gotten back to the rectory late one night when my friend Artie called from New York. He was on vacation and asked me to hop a plane and join him.

"I can't," I said. "I've got work to do."

"When's the last time you took a vacation?" he asked. "Come on. You can see some plays. You love plays. It'll be fun."

He talked me into it. When I got to the hotel, the desk man gave me a note. It said, "Meet me at Your Father's Mustache. In the Village. Seven o'clock."

I got there at seven. Artie wasn't there. I stood on the sawdust floor near the back and waited. A band in the front played banjos and a tuba and piano, and everybody in the room drank beer and sang songs like "Those were the days, my friend, we thought they'd never end." I looked at my watch. It was 7:30. Where was Artie?

I just stood there and watched everyone having fun. I noticed two girls sitting at a table against the wall. One was blonde, the other brunette. They were both pretty, but the brunette was stunning. She had long dark hair and wore a poncho like Clint Eastwood in *A Fistful of Dollars*. She was singing and swaying with such joy. I couldn't take my eyes off her.

And then I did something I had never done before. Here I was, a priest who had always kept the rules, and what did I do? I went and asked the bartender for a pitcher of beer. Then I walked over to the table and asked the girls, "Would you like some beer?" I probably sounded like Flounder in *Animal House*. I couldn't believe I was doing this. It was in slow motion.

They said, "Sure!" I sat in front of the brunette. She had the kind of face you could look at the rest of your life.

I noticed her eyes were different colors. One was hazel and speckled with green, and the other a cloudy blue. She asked me, "What do you do?"

"I'm a priest."

She laughed uncontrollably. That cinched it.

Artie came in and sat next to the blonde, and they sang while Vickie and I tried to talk over the music. After half an hour I asked her if she'd like to take a walk.

We walked around the Village for hours. It was one of those crisp October nights when the air is so clear you can see things in detail a mile away. Vickie told me about her cloudy blue eye, how she had fallen on a glass rabbit when she was a baby and the glass slashed her eye and blinded her. She told me how when the kids played games, she was always the bad guy or the monster, and that as she got older, adults looked at her and recoiled. "All I ever wanted," she said, "was to look like everybody else, or maybe find a prince who would love me like I am, and we'd have kids and live happily ever after in a house with a white picket fence."

"You're beautiful," I told her. I could tell she knew I meant it. "Would you like a dog too?" I asked.

"No. Just a prince."

I told her how I'd spent twelve years studying to be a priest and now after less than three years I was thinking about what it would be like to marry and have children. I had felt guilty about that feeling, but not about telling it to her. "Sometimes, when I wake up, I just lie there and look at the empty space next to me and think how wonderful it would be to wake up and see someone I love. Someone to hold and share life with. I even prayed to God once, if he'd let that happen, it would even be okay if she got sick and was dying before I did; I'd take care of her and love her right to the end. I promised God, if I break my commitment to being a priest, I will never break my commitment to her. Does that sound crazy?"

"My mama once told me," she said, "'when you meet the right person, you'll know, and you won't have to ask.'"

We walked and talked until two in the morning. We sat on the stoop of her tenement and talked some more. She told me that two guys actually wanted to marry her and she was conflicted. One of them was strong and the other gentle. She couldn't make up her mind. What did I think?

"I think you deserve to find someone who has both qualities."

She looked up at me. "I think I've found him."

I asked her something I hadn't asked anyone since Millie Brown in ninth grade. "May I kiss you?"

A year later we were married in St. Mark's in the Bowery, with a few friends and a gaggle of street urchins who were hanging around in the back and whom we invited to join us around the altar.

A year later Vickie's good eye got infected and the sick one had to be removed. We didn't have much money but were led to a Park Avenue surgeon, and after talking with Vickie, he said, "You deserve to look like everybody else." He did the operation without charging us. He then led us to a master craftsman of artificial eyes, and soon both of Vickie's dreams had come true.

Gratitude became the theme of her life. And, like the best wine, her life became richer with time.

I cannot count how many times she has said over the years, "Thank you, God!" Every time something good happens, she grabs my hand and says, "Let's pray. Thank you, God, for this blessing." Every time something adverse comes into our lives, we hold hands and say the Our Father and the Hail Mary and then, "Thank you, God." She often says right out of the blue: "Thank you, God, for my sweet-heart. Thank you for our wonderful boys."

It is now more than forty years later, and seven years since Vickie was diagnosed with early Alzheimer's. Her memory is going, but her refrain remains: "I've had two miracles in my life. How many people have even one? How could I not be grateful? I'm grateful to God for every moment."

Some people pay big bucks to go to seminars and learn how to live in the present moment. She does it naturally. And that is good for me too. I live on her clock. We don't think about the past, because it is gone. We don't think about the future, because it is unthinkable. We live in the present. And, as odd as it seems, we are having the time of our lives.

In the morning I work at my computer editing books while she sits behind me in the family room watching Regis, Rachel, and the girls of *The View*. If something funny is going on, I join her. In the afternoon we take a long walk in our neighborhood or along the Connecticut shoreline, or sometimes we'll drive to a neighborhood or town we've never seen before. We call that "Virgin Territory." While we're in the car, Vickie looks out the window, and whether it is sunny or cloudy, she exclaims (I kid you not), "The world is charged with the grandeur of God! Thank you, God." Or, from Psalm 118, "This is the day the Lord has made! Let us rejoice and be glad!"

When we walk in a neighborhood with mansions, I look at them with envy. She reminds me how blessed we are to have our comfy home. Then she cuts up this or that mansion just like everybody else. "Oh, that should be painted white," or "They need new shutters," or "Isn't that house too close to the road?" What could be more normal?

Sometimes we'll go to a matinee at the Loews Cineplex. Twelve big screens with stadium seating. When you're retired or semiretired like we are, there is nothing better than sitting together at a good movie with hardly anyone else there, eating hot buttered popcorn and sharing a twelve-ounce Diet Coke. I'll tell her when the story line changes and she'll say, "Shut up. I'm liking this."

After forty-two years she still surprises me. I was walking downstairs the other day, and out of the corner of my eye spotted her hiding around a corner, like a little girl, with a great big smile on her face. She couldn't wait to jump out. I let her; we laughed. She forgot it a minute later, but nothing real has really changed. Like our son Chris says, "It's all good."

Vickie would be a grateful person with or without her faith, but let me tell you, her faith has much to do with the way she sees the world. Where do you think her quotes come from? She goes to Mass every week and says the rosary every night, simply because they are expressions of gratitude she has always known. The chosen part is, "Thank you, God!"

Gratitude is the memory of the heart. It can't be erased.

Andrew Greeley

40

In Gratitude: Andrew Greeley

I wouldn't say the world is my parish, but my readers are my parish. And especially the readers that write to me. They're my parish. And it's a responsibility that I enjoy.
—ANDREW GREELEY

On November 7, 2008, on a windy day in Rosemont, Illinois, Fr. Andrew Greeley, one of the most creative Catholic thinkers of our time, wearing a Barack Obama baseball cap and a light raincoat, was stepping out of a cab. His raincoat caught in the door, the cab pulled away, and Greeley fell to the ground, smashing his head. He suffered a fractured skull, and his brain would not stop bleeding. Today, as I write this, he sits in a wheelchair in his apartment, no longer able to write the novels that used to write him, or initiate the witty repartee that delighted friends and confounded foes. His friend Fr. John Cusick says, "He still greets you with those deep blues that twinkle and that familiar smile of friendship and warmth. He has been a star in my heavens for all forty years of my priesthood.

No other priest has had a greater impact on me or on the church he loves so much than Andrew Greeley."

I am grateful to Fr. Greeley for fifty years of kindnesses. When I was twenty at St. Mary of the Lake Seminary, I received a handwritten letter from the thirty-three-year-old priest praising a short story I had written in the literary magazine *The New Southwell*. Fr. Greeley was already a famous priest, with two important books under his belt, *The Church and the Suburbs* and *Strangers in the House*. He not only encouraged me to continue writing but recommended the story to the editor of the popular Catholic magazine *The Critic*. The story wasn't published because a seminarian couldn't get anything published without the permission of the rector, who never gave permission. But Fr. Greeley's kindness to me, someone he didn't even know, thrilled me, and was an example I would follow years later in my publishing career.

When I was twenty-eight and had decided to leave the priesthood and move a thousand miles away to New York City, with no money and no job, and marry a girl I had known for four days in person and three months by phone, I went to see (now) Andy for advice. He lived in a small basement room at St. Ambrose Parish on the South Side. You entered by a side door and had to navigate towers of books that looked like the Chicago skyline. I sat in a chair across from him and told him the whole story. "So, the thing is," I said, "I don't know if it's going to work out, but *my whole being* is telling me this is what I have to do. If it was an actual voice there'd be an earthquake. I was wondering if you would do me a gigantic favor and write some of your editors and see if maybe I could get a job interview. I have to work for money now, and I thought I might be good at being a book editor. I love books. What do you think?"

Andy looked at me a long time, his chin resting on his fingers, then said, "I'll help you find a good psychiatrist."

We talked all night.

He wrote letters to the editors of Doubleday, MacMillan, and Sheed and Ward. They all interviewed me. None of them gave me a job because I had no experience. But Andy believed in me, and Vickie loved me, so I knocked on every door.

Just before my money ran out, a kind man at the Seabury Press hired me to write educational publications for the Episcopal Church. I was grateful for the job, but I wanted to be a book editor and soon realized that the only way that was going to happen was if I acquired books without being asked, in addition to the job I had, and presented the proposals to the publisher. My first presentation was for a book by a new friend named Richard Bolles, an Episcopal priest from New Jersey, whose sermons I edited for a subscription series called Selected Sermons. Dick had written a manuscript called *What Color Is Your Parachute?* for ex-clergy looking for a job. I proposed it, suggesting that anyone looking for a job would benefit from the book. The publisher turned it down. "It will never sell." Then I proposed a book called *The Sexual Celibate* by a Dominican named Donald Goergen, based on an article he had written for an obscure theology journal. Everybody thought I was nuts.

"There's a sexual revolution going on. Nobody's going to buy this." But they gave in, and the book was a best seller. So then the boss let me be a book editor, as long as I would also direct the department I was already in. No problem. I did both jobs so I could "make my bones" at the one I loved. I called Andy and asked him to write a book on the prayer of St. Patrick, *May the Wind Be at Your Back*, for a series I wanted to start on classic prayers. He said yes. He always said yes. The series got off to a fantastic start, and so did I.

We did a number of books together, some that I suggested and some he just sent me, and they were among the best books I would ever publish. *The Mary Myth* championed the feminine aspects of God before feminists did. *Neighborhood* sang a hymn to the value of community and presaged a future president. *The Communal Catholic* predicted what Catholics would be like in the future, and the prediction came true. *The Great Mysteries,* the first out-of-the-box catechism, is still in print and being taught after thirty-six years. Andy's books, his seminal articles, his work as a sociologist of religion, and his constructive criticism of the church made him a popular guest on talk shows. I remember when he was the sole guest on *The Phil Donahue Show.* A woman in the audience asked him, "If you're so critical of the church, why don't you just leave?" He famously said, "I *like* being Catholic!"

Years later I asked him to write a book called *I Like Being Catholic.* He wanted to but was too busy at the time. I asked again the next year. Andy said, "Look, you should write it." So I did. It was the most successful book I ever did.

On January 7, 1974, when Andy was forty-five and nowhere near his peak, *Time* magazine did a feature article on him. It began like this:

> "What is Andrew Greeley, anyway?" asked bewildered Theologian Tom Driver in a recent issue of *America*. "It might be a syndicate," he suggested. Dan Herr, president of Chicago's Thomas More Press, says, "I used to think there were four Greeleys. I was wrong. There are more than that."
>
> There indeed seem to be. The Rev. Andrew Greeley is, among other people, a Roman Catholic priest, a sociologist, a theologian, a weekly columnist (50 U.S. Catholic newspapers), the author of 40-odd books and, of late, a celibate sex expert. He is an informational machine gun who can fire off an article on Jesus to the *New York Times Magazine*, on ethnic groups to the *Antioch Review*, and on war to *Dissent*. This year he will write his first novel—about Chicago's Irish. "He's obsessive, compulsive, a workaholic," says Psychologist-Priest Eugene Kennedy, a close friend. "He's a natural resource. He should be protected under an ecological act."

Andrew Greeley was evolving into a new stage. It was as if the big black obelisk from *2001: A Space Odyssey* had appeared in his study and turned him into a new creation. He called me a year before the article: "Mike, I'm going to write novels now. I can reach more people that way. I want to tell stories of God's love. I know Seabury doesn't do fiction, but I was thinking you might help me on your own time and be my editor. I make a good salary from the University of Chicago and will pay you what you need. What do you say?"

I said, "Send me whatever you've got, and I will edit it for free. I'm writing my own book at night, so just give me time." He sent me two manuscripts: a literary novel called *Death in April* and a science-fiction novel whose name I forget, but the hero manned a spaceship called "The Mayor Daley," and I liked that. I left the first novel to the side and had fun with the second. The science-fiction novel didn't get published. *Death in April* was published by McGraw-Hill. It was Andy's first novel, and few people read it. He honed his skills on his own and found an agent. His next novel was *The Cardinal Sins*, read by millions of people around the world. A popular Catholic novelist was born.

Andy received criticism for his novels because they had mild sex scenes and some people couldn't tolerate the idea that a priest might know and write about such things. To Andy, sex was a sacramental sign of God's incredible love for us. *Everything* was a sacrament to him! He could see a movie and find five Christ figures in it, even if the movie was *Gidget Goes to Outer Space*. He was totally sincere about seeing God's love "lurking around corners." And he not only knew that "the chosen part" of sex between spouses was unselfish love but that unselfish love made for the best sex. A man doesn't have to have sex to know that this is so, or to celebrate it. Andy loved celebrating the good stuff.

Most of all he loved writing novels. "The story-teller is like God," he said. "The storyteller creates these characters. Falls in love with them, and then they won't act right." One of his lasting contributions is to show us that God is a Storyteller who writes straight the crooked lines of our lives, and that Catholicism is all about the stories. He writes in *The Sacramental Imagination*:

> I'm still a Catholic because of the stories I heard while I was growing up in the 1930s and forties in St. Angela parish on the west side of Chicago. Doctrine never exhausts the truth and the beauty of story. Thus, if I am asked whether I believe in the Madonna and Child or the Incarnation, my answer is that they are one and I believe in both. The doctrine of God become human is surely true, though it is an abstract statement of the truth contained in the story which begins with a journey from Nazareth to Bethlehem.

He also observed: "Religion has been passed down through the years by stories people tell around the campfire. Stories about God, stories about love. Practically speaking, your religion is the story you tell about your life."

Sometime in the late 1980s I got another phone call. "Mike, I've been writing a journal for a number of years and, I don't know, I think there might be some spiritual stuff in there people might find helpful. Would you mind taking a look and see if you think anything's worth publishing?" Three days later a box with hundreds of pages covering Andy's life and intimate thoughts over the past three years arrived like a package from a Unabomber intent on blowing *himself* up. It was extraordinary. It revealed a sensitive man who often suffered depression and *did* care what people thought about him, despite his public poses to the contrary, and who most of all wanted to love God and let people know that God was a Tremendous Lover who loved them as if he loved them alone and loved everyone as if all of them were one. I looked at the massive manuscript the same way Michelangelo looked at a block of marble: "It's not a block of marble. There's a lion in there!"

Andy did write about the spiritual life in his diaries, but he also talked about his joys and his conflicts, and he named names. It was no secret that he thought most American bishops were "morally and spiritually bankrupt"—he wrote about it in newspapers—and he told some juicy stories here. But I saw my main job as an editor was to protect Andy from himself. So I spent two weekends carving the marble down to what would be a small personal book called *Love Affair: A Prayer Journal.* It won a Catholic Book Award, and every couple of years I would do it again. These prayer journals were among his favorite books. I think most if not all of them are out of print now, but I'm grateful that I was able to work on them for him, his family and friends, and loyal readers.

His family and friends know that while Andy can show a dark side like everyone else, he is one of the kindest and most generous men you could ever know. Some priests have knocked him because he has earned lots of money and lives well, but they never praised him when he gave a million dollars to St. Mary of the Lake Seminary or to the University of Chicago or tried to give a million dollars to the archdiocese to support African American parishes rather than close them and his gift was refused by Cardinal John Cody. I know that one reason he kept on writing novels even when sales inevitably began to slip was not to live well but to keep on supporting others.

Andy's generosity is present even in his humor. Roberta Wilke, his assistant and friend for fifteen years, remembers walking into his office for the first time. *How am I to address this incredible human being?* she thought. *Dr. Greeley? Fr. Greeley? Rev. Greeley?* "When I posed the question, he looked at me quizzically, and said, 'Well, my name is Andy.' My other concern was that I'm not Catholic, so I thought it smart to lay that on the line right from the start. Andy glanced at me and said, 'Well, that's okay—you're a not a Republican, are you?' We had lost our young son the previous year, and I was pretty lost myself until Andy took me on board as his administrative assistant. Working for him enabled my healing."

Another Andrew Greeley I will always remember is the one who hated war, and wrote with fierce passion on the Iraq War in his *Chicago Sun Times* columns. He also wrote an extraordinary journal article on the just-war theory, and I put it at the end of one of the prayer journals even though it was a second thumb. Andy had the clarity and rigor of an Old Testament prophet, and I felt that the war essay deserved to be made public. In 2007, I asked Roberta to compile all the essays on the war he had written for the *Chicago Sun Times* from September 16, 2001 to March 30, 2007, and I published it as *Iraq: A Stupid, Unjust, Criminal War.* It was Andy's title, not mine, and while some of my colleagues thought the title was too harsh, I insisted it stay (one of the few times I've ever done that) rather than wait for a consensus. Reviewers perceived the book as the most comprehensive and incisive Catholic view of the Iraq War we would ever get. Historian Gary Wills wrote, "Andrew Greeley shows that Jesus is the Prince of Peace, not a Captain of War."

I could write a whole book about Andrew Greeley. I've exceeded the number of pages on this chapter that I allotted myself and feel as if I'm just getting started. Many of the good ideas you read in part 1 came first from Fr. Greeley. You can't go wrong by reading some of his books on Catholicism. When the history of the Catholic Church of the late twentieth century is written, there will be more references to his name than to anyone else's. Here are some brief, very Catholic, quotes from him you can find just by googling his name:

✢ The kernel is the belief that God is love and, in Catholicism, God's love is present in the world. It is in the sacraments, in the Eucharist, in our families, in our friends, in our neighborhood, and in forgiveness in the touch of a friendly hand, in a rediscovered love God is there.

✢ I don't think Jesus was an exclusivist. He said, and we believe, that he is the unique representation of God in the world. But that doesn't mean this is the only way God can work.

✢ I think Catholic Americans had better believe there's truth in all religions, because the Second Vatican Council said that. We don't believe that we have a monopoly on truth. We believe what we have is true, but it's not the whole truth. And we can learn a lot from the other religions if we listen to them respectfully.

✛ I think the only kind of acceptable evangelization is the evangelization of good example.

✛ Nobody puts constraints on God. She doesn't like it.

✛ What's more important? Life after death or birth control? What is more important? God's forgiving love or premarital sex?

✛ I have to say that I have no regrets about my decision to become a priest or about the major directions my ministry has taken me. I have been and am happy as a priest, and I have never been lonely. I could have used a bit more solitude.

I stay Catholic—countless Catholics stay Catholic— because Fr. Andrew Greeley has shown us why we *like* being Catholic. Thank you, Andy, and *ad multos annos!*

Come and see: agreeley.com

PART 3

Places

People are places that reveal the presence of God. Places are sacred spaces where God manifests through people. Everything begins with an idea that cannot help but express itself through people in places. Here are ten Catholic places that express ideas of truth, love, compassion, gratitude, peace, joy, oneness, goodness, wisdom, generosity, beauty, power, and tenderness by multiplying themselves through its people to other places throughout the world, even when those people stand still in the sacred space they inhabit. "You will receive power when the Holy Spirit breathes within you and you witness love in Jerusalem, and in all Judea and Samaria, and to the ends of the earth" (Acts 1:8). Jerusalem, Judea, and Samaria are *everywhere* because they are spiritual. You don't have to leave home to be a blessing to the world; you can do it on the sacred space on which you stand. Come and see ten places that soar over boundaries and transcend time.

Pentecost Mass, 2010, Old St. Patrick's Church, Chicago

41

Old St. Patrick's Parish

They devoted themselves to the teachings of Jesus and to community, to the breaking of the bread and to prayer. Awe came upon them and many wonders came to pass.

—ACTS 2:42–43

Old St. Patrick's Church faces Chicago's Loop to the east, or you could say the Loop faces Old St. Pat's, as does Indiana to the south, Wisconsin to the north, and most counties west to Iowa. Old St. Pat's is home to more than thirty-two hundred households in two hundred zip codes in every direction. "It is a community of communities," says Liz Collier of Evanston, "that come together in a unity of love."

Old St. Pat's has been a manifestation of love since Irish immigrants built it in the 1840s. It not only survived the Chicago Fire, but the flames took a detour and missed it by two blocks. The oldest public building in the city, it is also one of its liveliest. Its mission is to "serve the life and work of the laity in the world." More than two hundred lay leaders, under the spiritual direction of pastor

Fr. Tom Hurley, guide one thousand laypeople in more than ninety ministries serving more than twelve thousand active participants each year. Old St. Pat's sponsors an innovative Catholic school on two campuses and a vibrant outreach to young adults; sends volunteers to poor parishes in Chicago, Mississippi, Haiti, and Latin America; and hosts the "World's Largest Block Party" each July. You think it's something when Mayor Daley dyes the river green on St. Patrick's Day? Check out the festivities at Old St. Pat's, when over two nights more than twenty thousand people gather in the streets surrounding the church to celebrate life in the city!

It wasn't always this way. In 1960 an expressway split the church from its neighborhood the way a guillotine severs a head. The parish couldn't breathe, and the building faced death by demolition. By 1983, Old St. Pat's had only four registered members. Enter Fr. Jack Wall. The new pastor had a vision of church as a thriving community of Christians worthy of the same observation that Tertullian made in the second century: "See how they love one another!" And he had a plan. The Loop was next door, so he made Old St. Pat's a retreat for working professionals, created the Crossroads Center for Faith and Work to empower evangelization in the workplace, invited business people to worship with the neighboring poor, invited the neighboring poor to help shape the church programs, and brought in his friend, the charismatic Fr. John Cusick, to reach out to young adults who believed in God but did not have confidence in the church. Within five years the four registered members soared to more than a thousand families. Old St. Patrick's opened the first new Catholic grammar school in the archdiocese in more than twenty-five years. And the parish kept flourishing like the biblical tree that bears good fruit.

Old St. Pat's is at the center of the city and in the heart of Catholicism. "We are a mystery religion," says parishioner Mary Anne Moriarity, "a people of faith who believe in an imminent, intimate, loving God. We are a people who believe in Jesus as the one who so believed and so loved this God that nothing and no one would keep him from that union. We are a people who believe in the Spirit who lives within us and in whom we live. That is the message we receive over and over again at Old St. Pat's—in the celebrations of our liturgies, in our deeply spiritual homilies, in our sacred music, and in and with a community of believers fully alive in Christ."

The chosen part of any parish is the biblical virtue of hospitality. And Old St. Pat's practices Christian hospitality as well as any parish in any place at any time. Everyone is welcome. Everyone is invited to participate. Everyone has a part to play in the drama of salvation and the comedy of community. Everyone has a gift, and every gift is valued. Bob Kolatorowicz has been a parishioner for more than twenty years and directs the parish's adult spirituality and social-justice programs. He recalls when he was a college student and came across a greeting card that had "the most Catholic words ever uttered." To him it symbolizes the grace of Old St. Pat's.

What caught my eye was the image of a beaming Charley Brown holding an open envelope and his own invitation to a party. Next to his round head, floating in a dialogue bubble, was that most sublime Catholic phrase: "We've *all* been invited!"

The often excluded Charley Brown was smiling and proclaiming the good news, "We've been invited! We've *all* been invited!"

It has stayed with me ever since. Whatever it is that God has in mind for us, it is not just for *some* of us; it is for *all of us*. Now, I know it's a little over the top to read too much into a greeting card, but that smile on Charley Brown's face? I don't think it's there just because *he's* been invited. In my religious imagination I like to believe that his smile reflects the joy and peace of learning that we've *all* been invited.

The good news about Old St. Pat's is that we're always trying to do this better. Whether it's a commitment to welcoming newcomers, exploring interreligious dialogue, addressing immigration issues, or the formation of a new gay and lesbian outreach, it's always inspiring to see so many people at Old St. Pat's willing to lead each other into a deeper, more holy communion. And why not? It's all just an echo of those most Catholic words ever uttered: "We've *all* been invited!"

At Old St. Pat's, diverse members of the Body of Christ gather in the name of Jesus, not their own names, and in sacred space, not their own space, to worship, not as many but as one. Their differences are the gifts they give one another. They learn to be grateful for one another's blessings. What blesses one, blesses all.

Fr. Hurley nails it on the parish Web page: "We challenge each other to go forth and transform the world into a holier, peaceful, and more just place to live. We invite you to join us for Sunday Mass, as well as countless programs and activities throughout the week! *We're All Invited* to Old St. Patrick's Church!"

Come and see: oldstpats.org

Open field at Gethsemani

42

The Abbey of Our Lady of Gethsemani

Erase yourself, utterly.
—Zen Master

Be still, and know that I am God.
—Psalm 46:10

The Abbey of Our Lady of Gethsemani, a place of prayer in a sacred space near the Allegheny Mountains, is everywhere and nowhere. You can get there from here without ever leaving home, but more about that later. You can also fly to Louisville, rent a car, and take Highway 245 to Bardstown, where you'll marvel at the magnificent St. Joseph Proto-Cathedral, a national landmark, before moving on to Culvertown, where you'll spot a Kwik Mart. Drive three miles out of town with the windows open so you can smell the sweet bluegrass, but be careful not to pass the entranceway to the Abbey. Take a left, but drive slowly so you can appreciate the looming white monastery against a sky so rich and blue you could scoop it with a spoon. Park and go to the visitor's center. You'll know it by the unassuming sign that says, "Let all guests that come be received like Christ."

The Trappist monks who live at the Abbey practice Christian hospitality, but the chosen part of their lives is prayer. Keeping a schedule established in 1848, the monks get up each morning at 3:00 and begin their day by chanting the Divine Office at 3:15 with Vigils, and end it at 7:30 p.m. with Compline. Inbetween they work, eat, play, meditate, celebrate Eucharist, and sing other parts of the Office. Whatever they are doing, they endeavor to live in the conscious presence of God. The theme of their lives, the chosen part, is "pray always" (Luke 21:36).

When I went to Trip Advisor recently on the internet and typed "Abbey of Gethsemani," I found this single visitor's review:

SERENE PLACE WITH PHENOMENAL BOURBON FUDGE! We stopped here on a rainy afternoon and had a delightful visit. Went to the Chapel but missed the evensong. Love the Bourbon Fudge made by the monks and sold in the gift shop. All our friends will be receiving this for Christmas this year!

Indeed, making fantastic fudge, cheese, and fruitcake is one way the monks support themselves. I have a friend, John Raub, who lived there for many years and wrote a book called *Who Told You That You Were Naked?* Each Christmas he sent us a delicious fruitcake he had made.

By New Year's I could have written a book called *Who Told You That You Were Fat?* The monks have a store at the Abbey and a mail-order business as well.

The Abbey also offers retreats. Laity and clergy from all over the country come to get away from their noisy schedules and get in tune with the infinite for a few days. In the words of the most famous Trappist, Thomas Merton, Gethsemani is a place apart "to entertain silence in the heart and listen to the voice of God—to pray for your own discovery."

Merton, the most important Catholic writer of the twentieth century, lived at Gethsemani for twenty-seven years. Encouraged by the Abbot to write his autobiography, *The Seven Storey Mountain,* he went on to write dozens of books on topics ranging from prayer to world peace. He was one of the first Catholics to introduce Eastern wisdom to Western readers, and Gethsemani has since become a world center of interreligious dialogue. But most of all, Merton introduced all readers to the value of Christian contemplation, a way of prayer that happens when we stop thinking and hear the still, small voice of God (1 Kings 19:12). Long before Americans were discovering Zen (meditation) and satori (enlightenment), Merton was shedding light on contemplation and understanding our true nature, or being in heaven while still on earth. The mystic Meister Eckhart wrote that in contemplation, "We see God with the same eyes that God sees us." *The Catechism of the Catholic Church* refers to Jesus in contemplation: "I look at him and he looks at me." Merton wrote, "The Christian life—and especially the contemplative life—is a continual discovery of Christ in new and unex-pected places."

Merton wrote famously about a moment of satori, or encounter with Christ, that came to him while he was standing in a shopping district in downtown Louisville:

> I was suddenly overwhelmed with the realization that I loved all those people, that they were mine and I theirs, that we could not be alien to one another even though we were total strangers. It was like walking from a dream of separateness, of spurious self-isola-tion in a special world, the world of renunciation and supposed holiness. . . . There is no way of telling people that they are all walking around shining like the sun. . . . There are no strangers! . . . The gate of heaven is everywhere."

We can know this, too, without going to the Abbey of Our Lady of Gethsemani. The sacred space just beyond Bardstown, Kentucky, is within us and all around us. All the time, and in no time at all. Gethsemani is an exem-plar of a chosen part of Catholic prayer: being still, los-ing interest in our thoughts, and letting God do all the talking. The monks teach us that whether we are singing or making fruitcake, picking berries or picking at a key-board, working on a farm or in a skyscraper, driving our kids to school or in a truck going up I-95, we can live in conscious awareness of the presence of God.

We can each sit in the empty chair pictured at the beginning of this chapter, wherever we are, and view a world waiting to be transformed. The world before us becomes a new creation when we see it with the same eyes with which God sees us. We don't make that happen; God does. "It is the Father, living in me, who does the work" (John 14:10). There's a story about a Zen fishmonger who reportedly became enlightened but still peddled fish and still smelled of fish, and his friends asked, "What's so great about your life now?" He answered, "Well, everything is exactly the same as it was before, except that wherever I go, the dead trees come to life." Jesus told his disciples that even the stones could speak (Luke 19:40). Merton said, "Life is this simple: we are living in a world that is absolutely transparent and the divine is shining through it all the time. This is not just a nice story or a fable, it is true."

The fruit of contemplation is awareness of the divine. Contemplation is not thinking about God. It is—if only for a moment—suddenly, *God thinking us.*

Merton and the monks of Gethsemani remind us that contemplation takes patience, understanding, and know-how. Merton's canon of books includes more than a dozen on the contemplative way. He sheds light on what it is and how to prepare ourselves for the moment when God comes just like that and leaves a memory that lasts forever.

When we are alone on a starlit night, when by chance we see the migrating birds in autumn descending on a grove of junipers to rest and eat; when we see children in a moment when they are really children, when we know love in our own hearts; or when, like the Japanese poet, Basho, we hear an old frog land in a quiet pond with a solitary splash—at such times the awakening, the turning inside out of all values, the "newness," the emptiness and the purity of vision that make themselves evident, all these provide a glimpse of the cosmic dance.

I confess: I have never taken a plane to Louisville. But I have been to Gethsemani. Thomas Merton gave me directions.

Come and see: monks.org (Gethsemani) and *Thomas Merton: Essential Writings*, compiled by Christine M. Bochen

A Sister of Charity, early 20th century (Duncan Sprott)

43

Catholic Charities

*I was hungry and you gave me food. I was thirsty and you
gave me drink. I was naked and you gave me clothing. I
was sick and you took care of me. I was in prison and you
visited me. Truly I tell you, just as you did it to one of the least
of these who are members of my family, you did it to me!*
—MATTHEW 25:34–40

A century before President George W. Bush called for
"faith-based initiatives," Catholic Charities, often in partnership with government, was feeding the hungry, sheltering the homeless, nurturing abandoned babies, protecting
neglected children, welcoming refugees, helping immigrants assimilate, caring for the sick, and burying the dead.

Catholic Sisters were practicing heroic works of mercy
in 1727, fifty years before the Declaration of Independence.
They opened, managed, and served in hospitals, orphan-
ages, and schools. Twenty-one of the seventy-seven charities for children established in the U.S. before the middle
of the nineteenth century were Catholic. What Mother

Teresa said 250 years later was their mantra as well: "The child is God's gift to the family. Each child is created in the special image and likeness of God for greater things, to love and to be loved." The chosen part of Catholic Charities has always been our dignity as children of God. We are all members of one body, and what happens to the least of us happens to all of us.

When Catholic Charities united as an organization in 1910, the United States was much like our nation today. Voters wanted reform, immigrants wanted opportunity, and technology was changing everything. The richer were richer and the poor poorer. More than half of the Catholics in the U.S. had been born in foreign lands and were growing up in squalor. The Church understood that charity and justice were crucial aspects of its mission as well as obligations of citizenship. So did government, which has helped to support countless faith-based services since the nineteenth century.

Today the Catholic Charities network includes more than seventeen hundred agencies across the United States. It is the second-largest social-service provider in the country, surpassed only by the federal government. Its 240,000 volunteers and staff serve more than 9 million people, regardless of religious, social, or economic backgrounds. Ninety percent of its donations go directly to programs and services. Lay administrators lead 90 percent of diocesan charity organizations. A 2010 study ranked Catholic Charities number six in "The Cone Top 10 Non-Profit Power Brands," joining other household names on the list, such as United Way, Red Cross, and Salvation Army.

Beneath the impressive statistics are inspiring stories, nine million of them. Catholic Charities of Colorado Springs provides a compassionate adoption program. Its website introduces us to a young woman who placed her baby for adoption:

> When I found out I was pregnant I was scared and wasn't sure what to do. I was scared to be judged because I didn't know who the father was. I didn't have a job at the time and all I wanted was what was best for this Little One.
>
> I felt from the beginning Little One needed a two-parent home. I checked out several agencies and I immediately felt a connection with Catholic Charities. I didn't know a lot about adoption, so I didn't know what was in store for me and my mom, who was a great support.
>
> I walked in closed minded, though during hours of counseling they explained the difference between open and closed adoption. I chose to pick the adoptive parents and meet with them. I will call them Annie and Jeff. I wanted Annie and Jeff to be a part of this process, as much as they could. I asked them to be in the birthing room with me. They came to the hospital and were by my side, with Catholic Charities and my mom.
>
> I ended up having to have a c-section and hospital policy allows only one person in the room. I believe

God's hand was in this from the beginning because he changed the hospital policy and my mom, Annie and Jeff were all allowed in there with me. I believe the Little One came into this world to be a blessing for another family.

During counseling we learned bonding was very important with the Little One. Annie and Jeff stayed at the hospital after Little One arrived so the bonding could begin.

Catholic Charities was there as well to help with the process. In my heart I knew I made the right decision. Catholic Charities and Annie and Jeff were there for me all the way and are still with me today. I still have a great relationship with Annie and Jeff and Little One. I thank God, my mom, Annie and Jeff and Catholic Charities for all the support I received. Thank you Catholic Charities for helping me make the most important decision in my life.

Fr. Charles Rubey has directed programs for Catholic Charities of Chicago for forty years. He has spent much of his life comforting the sorrowful who have lost loved ones to suicide. "The beatitudes talk about those who mourn," he says, "and I am grateful that I have been able to reach out to them and bring some comfort in their journey of grief. I don't have the answers; I just try to be there for them. God has become more of a mystery to me than ever. He has become more enticing, more elusive, yet closer. I spend time each day trying to experience the presence of this holy Mystery. It's like trying to hold mercury in my hand. My faith assures me that someday this Mystery will consume me and I'll be dissolved in it. At that moment any questions I've had about life and death won't matter."

In 1987, Pope John Paul II addressed all who labor in the vineyard of Catholic Charities from San Antonio, Texas. He speaks for all of us:

> We have seen how Catholic Charities and all its colleague associations have lent God their own flesh—their hands and feet and hearts—so that his work may be done in our world. For your long and persevering service—creative and courageous, and blind to the distinctions of race or religion—you will certainly hear Jesus' words of gratitude: "You did it for me!" So gather, transform, and serve! By working for a society which fosters the dignity of every human person, not only are you serving the poor but you are renewing the founding vision of this nation under God! And may God reward you abundantly!

Come and see: catholiccharitiesusa.org and *Think and Act Anew: How Poverty in America Affects Us All and What We Can Do about It* by Larry Snyder

Convent of the Sacred Heart, Greenwich, Connecticut

44

Catholic Schools

We need to learn to see things in the light of eternity.
—SR. JANET ERSKINE STUART, RSCJ,
THE EDUCATION OF CATHOLIC GIRLS, 1912

The whole conversation today about values in education
emulates what's been happening in Catholic schools.
The rest of the country's coming around to what Catholic
educators have always known.
—COKIE ROBERTS, GRADUATE, STONE RIDGE COUNTRY
DAY SCHOOL OF THE SACRED HEART, 1960

Bart Simpson famously asked his mom, Marge, "Can we go Catholic so we can get wafers and booze?" Marge does put him in a Catholic school when he gets kicked out of the public school, and Bart not only likes it but begins to embrace Catholicism. His dad, Homer, rushes to take him out, but by evening he is converted. Hilarity, and inspiration, ensues. Catholic schools have that effect on you.

Holy Rosary is a real Catholic school in Darlington, Wisconsin. Cody, grade two, likes it too. "It's a great school," he says. "We learn about God. We have penny wars to help people. We collect food for the food pantry. We help and share God with other people." Catholic schools do that to you.

Tim Russert, the late, great journalist, wrote about how his dad, Big Russ, "worked two jobs all his life so his four kids could go to Catholic school, and those schools changed my life. They not only taught me to read and write, but also to tell right from wrong." We knew that every time we watched Russert on *Meet the Press*.

Catholic schools make up the largest private school system in the world. Four of the top-ten largest school districts in the U.S. are Catholic: the Archdioceses of Los Angeles, Chicago, New York, and Boston. In 2010, more than four million students attended fourteen thousand Catholic elementary, middle, and high schools in the United States. Nearly a third of the students are minorities, and 15 percent are non-Catholic. The student/teacher ratio is 14:1. The average tuition cost for elementary schools is $3,383. More than 95 percent of all Catholic schools, K to 12, offer parents nongovernmental financial assistance.

Catholic education in the U.S. goes back to at least 1606, when Franciscans opened a school in what is now St. Augustine, Florida. The first established school in the Thirteen Colonies was a Catholic school in Maryland in 1640. Catholics were definitely a minority in this country's beginning, and the targets of bigotry, but four hundred years later Americans regard Catholic schools as a gift to the nation. Nearly two thousand Catholic schools have a waiting list for admission.

The United States is also blessed with more than two hundred Catholic colleges and universities, including many prestigious law, medical, and nursing schools, and some of the highest-ranked schools in the nation: Georgetown, Notre Dame, Boston College, Holy Cross, and St. John's. Georgetown was the first, founded by the Jesuits in 1789. Wyoming Catholic College is the newest, founded in 2007. *U.S. News & World Report, Barron's, Time* and *Money* consistently rate Catholic colleges as "Best Buy" or "Best Value" or simply among the "Best" schools, and the Templeton Foundation time and again cites them on its honor roll of "Character-Building Schools."

Catholic colleges and universities are mission driven, striving to maintain their Catholic identity as well as academic excellence. They not only teach *about* the faith but also offer students opportunities to *express* their faith through liturgies, retreats, and ministry projects. Caldwell College in New Jersey, for instance, is rooted in the Dominican tradition and is "committed to promoting the Gospel message of truth." Students not only have an array of religious services; they also may volunteer to serve meals to the hungry in Newark, distribute clothing and blankets to the homeless in New York, work with physically challenged teenagers at Horizon High School for Cerebral Palsy, or cheer up old folks at a local senior residence. The chosen part of all Catholic colleges is Jesus' challenge to go forth and teach what he taught us, if necessary, even by using words.

While everyone knows about the Society of Jesus' (SJ) contributions to higher education in America, few of us know about the contributions of the Society of the Sacred Heart (RSCJ) to prekindergarten through high school education. The women of RSCJ are the yin to the Jesuits' yang. The quote that starts out this chapter comes from one of them, Sr. Janet Erskine Stuart, one of the leading educators in our history. Founded by St. Madeleine Sophie Barat in 1800, the Society has a presence in forty-five countries but is admired in the U.S. for their twenty-one outstanding high schools. Their alumni include a Who's Who of American Women ranging from Cokie Roberts to Lady Gaga. The schools go to great lengths to find grants for students in need.

Sr. Joan Magnetti, RSCJ, is another notable graduate of a Sacred Heart school. A distinguished educator, she has served thirty-two years as headmistress of two Sacred Heart schools, and is now executive director of the six inner-city Bridgeport schools of the Diocese of Bridgeport. Like Janet Erskine Stuart before her, Joan Magnetti views the chosen part of Catholic education as "seeing things in the light of eternity." Thomas Aquinas wrote that the goal of the Christian life is an act of seeing, and contemporary theologian Robert Barron affirms, "Catholicism is above all a way of seeing."

Sr. Magnetti asks, "What is a good way for Catholic educators to pass on that vision today? The way Catholicism has always taught best: through stories."

I asked her to tell me one.

Well, I am a collector of Indian Storyteller Dolls from the American Southwest. These dolls represent the storyteller who arrived at the village and gathered the children to tell them the eternal truths, the ways of the tribe, the stories of ancestors, reverence for creation, and how to preserve and love the things of the tribe.

As a Catholic educator, I, too, told stories: Gospel stories, playground stories, stories of saints, of founders and foundresses. Sure, I worked vigilantly to stabilize and diversify enrollment, hired and let go staff, raised money, worried over finances and septic systems, town-and-gown issues. But still, my favorite form of leadership was in the stories, the telling of stories. Hopefully, I led the children to timeless values such as kindness, the holiness of the other—"By the way, girls, that is why you hold the door for each other"—the righteousness of honest living, the value of church and community, and the adage so beloved by generations of Sacred Heart students, straight from the gospel, "[From] those to whom much is given much is required."

My favorite stories now—and they still make me weep—are the stories of the students I taught. They are stories of huge heroism on the part of Catholic youth who not only study hard but volunteer on behalf of the poor, who tough their ways through divorced parents or their own childhood cancer. Forget the misleading headlines about the selfishness of the new generations. These young people have taught me a bravery that has humbled me. They have made me realize that *they* were the real storytellers, not me. Now they tell their own stories to the next generation! There is nothing more Catholic than its stories. No wonder Jesus taught in parables!

Talking with Sr. Magnetti makes me grateful for my own Catholic education. Her enthusiasm for today's students almost makes me want to go back to school.

Come and see: ncea.org and rscj.org

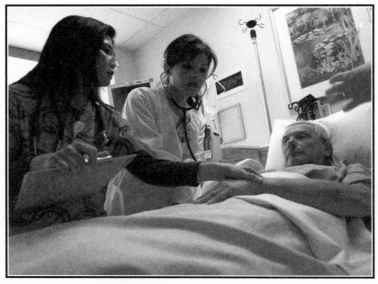

St. Joseph Hospital, Orange, California

45

Catholic Hospitals

*When you leave your prayers for the bedside of
a patient, you are leaving God for God. Looking
after the sick is praying.*
—St. Vincent De Paul (1581–1660)

The first hospital I was ever in was Columbus Hospital in
Chicago. Founded in 1905 by Mother Cabrini, the first
American citizen to be made a saint, the hospital was
within a lion's roar of the Lincoln Park Zoo. I was sixteen, and my appendix had burst. Pete Junius comman-
deered a jalopy (I don't know if Pete had a license) and
raced me to the hospital. They operated and wrapped up
my torso like a mummy. I spent three lovely days there,
looking out a window to the lakefront and appreciating the sweet encouragement of a Candy Striper named
Penny, who sat by my side and held my hand. I lost my
heart in Columbus Hospital.

Columbus made its bones by serving the sick and poor
in ethnic neighborhoods that stretched from the lake to

the near suburbs. On September 28, 2001, it was forced to close its doors because of a devastating illness striking all hospitals: the Profit Plague. Real-estate interests anticipated its death and rushed to its bedside. Today what was Columbus Hospital is an unfinished luxury-condo complex, a victim of the housing bubble.

The first New York City hospital I was in was St. Vincent's in Greenwich Village. Founded in 1849 by the Sisters of Charity, the hospital took care of anyone who was sick, especially the poor, and became the busiest hospital in Manhattan. I was twenty-nine, new to the city, and on a snowy day with drifts up to six feet had tried to leap over a curbside puddle the size of a landing strip. I didn't make it, and landed up to my ankles in icy water. My heart flipped into tachycardia and fibrillation, pounding about two hundred irregular beats a minute. I got to the hospital, and for what seemed like an eternity lay on a gurney in a bustling hallway with other patients lined up the same way in front of me and behind me as far as I could see. I thought of the railroad yard in *Gone with the Wind*, and waited for Vivian Leigh. Nurses and doctors did take care of me and everyone else that day, as they would twenty-four hours a day, seven days a week, until they, too, were forced to close their doors forever on April 30, 2010.

The hospital that had treated the shivering passengers of the *Titanic* in 1912 and the trembling victims of the Twin Towers on 9/11, as well as mended a billion broken bones and beaten hearts, could no longer make it in an HMO world where money was king. Today all the patients who would have been going to St. Vincent's are overflowing the emergency room of its longtime neighbor, Bellevue Hospital, to the point that it's like an entire town trying to fit into a phone booth.

The medical crisis in the U.S. affects every hospital and every family, but one thing is certain: Catholic hospitals will be a major part of the solution, as they have been since the beginning of our great nation.

The Ursuline Sisters opened the first hospital in what would become the continental United States in New Orleans in 1728. In 1823 the Sisters of Charity, under the inspiration of Mother Elizabeth Ann Seton, the first native-born citizen to be made a saint, opened an infirmary in Baltimore. During the Civil War, when more than six hundred thousand men died and even more were maimed, Catholic Sisters were the only trained and organized nurses in the country. The Sisters of Charity, Sisters of St. Joseph, Sisters of Mercy, and Sisters of the Holy Cross were on the front lines caring for the wounded and dying. President Lincoln praised them for their heroic dedication. For almost three hundred years Catholic sisters took the lead in providing health care to soldiers, immigrants, the rich, the poor, and the middle-class. Their mission was, and is, the healing mission of Jesus.

While the numbers of religious women are declining, the Catholic Church remains one of the largest health-care providers in the United States. More than six hundred Catholic hospitals treat more than 90 million patients each year. Eleven of the nation's forty largest systems are Catholic. The largest is Ascension Health, based in St. Louis, with sixty-seven acute-care hospitals in twenty states and the District of Columbia, sponsored by the Daughters of Charity National Health System, the Sisters of St. Joseph of Carondelet, the Congregation of St. Joseph in Cleveland, and others. A 2010 analysis from Thomson Reuters shows that Catholic and other church-owned health systems "are significantly more likely to provide higher quality performance and efficiency to the communities served than investor-owned systems." The chosen part of Catholic hospitals is Jesus' mission of love and healing in the world.

St. Joseph Hospital in Orange, California, is one of the top Catholic hospitals and systems in the country. Katie Skelton, the vice president of Patient Care Services and chief nursing officer, has been a nurse for more than thirty years, mostly in public hospitals. Coming to St. Joseph, she says, was like coming home.

> While the medical and administrative challenges were the same, I soon realized that the culture in this Catholic hospital was different from any other place I had ever worked. There is a connectedness amongst the people that I have not experienced before. It transcends the physical and emotional. There is a spiritual connectedness to each other and to those we serve. You can feel it from the bedside

to the boardroom. New employees and visitors to the campus recognize that something is "different" here but they can't yet name it. I think it takes years to understand and appreciate the depth and connectedness of this remarkable community of people within this Catholic hospital. There is a willingness and commitment of the people to STAND WITH. Good times or bad times. Celebrating a wonderful achievement or burying a loved one. This STAND WITH happens every day, multiple times, multiple places, all across the campus.

Nurses at St. Joseph are encouraged to write clinical narratives, stories. These are real nurse-patient stories that can demonstrate a variety of human needs, emotions, challenges, and caring behaviors. Through writing and reflecting, nurses can gain insight into their own approach to care and also share this learning with others. One of my favorite stories, and one that demonstrates STANDING WITH, was written by one of our Women's Services nurses.

Mary, RN, tells the story of caring for a 38-year-old Hispanic woman who was admitted to the hospital during her fourth miscarriage. Mary wasn't supposed to be her nurse. She already had her full assignment of patients. But when Mary realized that this patient and her husband spoke very little English, and that she had the best command of Spanish of all the nurses working that day, she insisted on making a switch. She sat at the bedside of her patient and the husband and heard their sad story. For ten years they had been trying to have children. This was the furthest along she had ever carried a pregnancy. They had had such great hopes for this child. Mary listened, she cried, she educated, she comforted. She tended to the physical needs, made sure both patient and husband understood what to expect when their tiny baby would arrive. She stayed with them as their fourth child was delivered, too tiny to survive. She wrapped the tiny infant in a blanket, asked if they wanted to hold their daughter and be with her. She asked them if they wanted pictures of their baby. She gave them time. She was present for them. She asked if they wanted her to baptize their daughter. They did. They chose Mary's name as their daughter's middle name. Mary stayed with the family well into the next shift, as STANDING WITH does not end at a shift change.

The times they are a-changing. But one thing doesn't change: we live; we die. During that time in the middle we will probably find ourselves like the man in the picture that opens this chapter. We may be in a Catholic hospital or a public hospital or a private hospital. But if we're fortunate, whoever cares for us, whether they know it or not, will be imbued with the spirit that motivated Mother Cabrini and Mother Seton and all the sisters that followed. Henri Nouwen sums it up:

The friend who can be silent with us in a moment of despair or confusion, who can stay with us in an hour of grief and bereavement, who can tolerate not knowing . . . not *healing*, not curing . . . that is a friend who cares.

Come and see: chausa.org (Catholic Health Association of the U.S.A.) and sjo.org (St. Joseph Hospital and Health System)

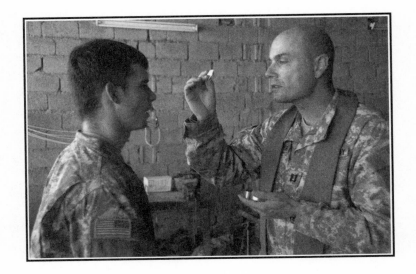

46

The Catholic Church Extension Society

The Church doesn't have a mission. Mission has a Church.
—JOHN J. WALSH, M.M.

In the early twentieth century, as Italian, Irish, and German immigrants were building churches in Boston, New York, and Chicago, nine out of ten rural communities didn't even have a chapel. Catholics in what we now call "fly-over country" practiced their faith without a roof over their heads or even a priest. In 1905, Fr. Francis Clement Kelley (1870–1948) aimed to change this. He had just returned from a tour of parishes on the Midwestern frontier and was appalled by their squalid state. He proposed to Chicago archbishop James Quigley the creation of an organization that would raise funds among Catholics across America to help build faith and foster self-sustaining Catholic communities in these poor, far-flung, and remote places. Together, they founded the Catholic Church Extension Society.

Catholic Extension sought to achieve in the wilds of Wyoming, South Dakota, and Mississippi what missionaries from the Society of the Divine Word and Maryknoll (who were traveling to China, Latin America, and Africa to build local churches) were achieving internationally: to strengthen the Catholic faith in places where it was struggling to gain a foothold. However, Catholic Extension took a different approach. Rather than send missionaries into the field, the organization listened to requests from the priests, sisters, and laypeople already living in dioceses that could not sustain themselves without support. It then awarded grants to these missionaries and their communities to help them build faith, inspire hope, and ignite lasting change. For more than one hundred years Catholic Extension has continued to be a stalwart partner, a connection to the universal church—consistently affirming that they are in communion with Catholics across America who care about them.

When Hurricane Katrina ripped through the Gulf Coast and turned towns such as Lake Charles, Waveland, and Houma into ghost towns, volunteers from 245 Catholic parishes in 109 dioceses partnered with parishes in the stricken areas to help them rebuild. On television we saw volunteers flocking to the devastated areas, and our hearts warmed. What we didn't see on TV was the work of Catholic Extension in funding an unprecedented Parish Partnership Program with Gulf Coast communities in mission dioceses that encouraged young people to leave their comfortable lives and jump into the lives of people in danger.

Nobody will probably ever see Sr. Kathleen Kane on television. Sister ministers to Native Americans in outlying parishes in Montana, where many of them don't even have televisions. She travels to three different communities stretched over five thousand square miles, where people struggle with 75 percent unemployment and inadequate housing, food, clothing, and transportation. Sister Kathleen is one of many missionaries who bring God's comfort to America's poor with the support of Catholic Extension.

Few people could ever even *find* Fr. Tom Brundage, a pastor in Palmer, Alaska, who drives 150 icy miles through twisting mountain roads to celebrate Mass for the Catholics of Holy Family Parish in Glennallen. On one visit his car broke down, and he waited fourteen hours in subzero temperatures before being rescued. But he got there safely, and his people rejoiced. So did Catholic Extension, which provides critical financial support to Fr. Brundage and hundreds of churches just like the one in Glennallen.

Fr. Ricardo Villarreal serves a vast Hispanic congregation scattered all over the Yakima Valley of Washington. He celebrates seven Masses on weekends, two in English and five in Spanish. He baptizes thirty babies a month and oversees religious-education classes for six hundred students. Fr. Villarreal is grateful for his grant from Catholic Extension and gratified to see the faith passed on to a younger generation. "People here work hard and pray hard," he says. "You'll see them working fourteen hours a day to put food on their family's table. I am blessed to be among them."

Sister Noreen McLaughlin and Sister Amy Kistner also know about poverty and the courage of the people they serve at the Church of the Good Shepherd in Campton, Kentucky. Median income for families at this little parish in the foothills of Appalachia is at the Census Bureau's low watermark for a family of four. The child poverty rate is 55 percent. The sisters teach and live the gospel. They host a monthly luncheon for cancer survivors and assist families each Christmas with food and warm coats and toys for the children. They distribute much-needed toiletries not covered by food stamps, items such as shampoo and toothpaste. Again, Catholic Extension and its donors make these apparently little things possible. Put them side by side, and they make a mountain range of love longer than the Appalachians.

Catholic Extension is the Little Engine That *Does*. Perhaps the least-known Catholic charity in the United States, it is definitely one of the most needed and most effective. The Society provides training and teaching materials for religious education in remote areas in fifty-six dioceses. It provides salary subsidies for more than four hundred U.S. missionaries in forty dioceses so that they can focus on helping people in their communities become more self-sufficient. It sees to the building and repair of churches—more than twelve thousand so far—in places tourists don't often visit. It supports campus ministry programs at ninety state or private colleges in thirty-eight dioceses. Thinking of the future of the Church, the Society helps defray the cost of tuition, books, and liturgical supplies for more than four hundred seminarians from the mission dioceses so they, too, can one day return to their communities as missionaries in their own backyards. It also supports the vocation work of the Archdiocese for the Military Services, helping train priests to serve as chaplains to our troops on U.S. bases as well as overseas. In fact, since its founding, Catholic Extension has not only awarded almost $500 million to help countless communities more fully participate in the larger mission of the Catholic Church; it also has given countless donors the opportunity to be in mission as well.

"Catholics in America hear Christ's message to do God's work in the world when they refuse to let the harsh realities of poverty and isolation keep their brothers and sisters from experiencing the gift of a vibrant faith realized in a loving church community," says Fr. Jack Wall, president of Catholic Extension. "We make it possible for everyone to experience the deepest truth of our faith that we are one with God and each other by linking donors' lives, their prayers, and their financial support to people who are poor in material goods but rich in faith. Together, we all give testimony to the power of Christ to transform our lives, our families, our communities, and our nation."

The next time somebody complains about priests, I hope I remember to tell them about Fr. Tom Brundage in Alaska and Fr. Ricardo Villarreal in Washington. If someone diminishes the impact of nuns, I hope I remember to tell them about Sisters Noreen McLaughlin and Amy Kistner in Kentucky, and Sr. Kathleen Kane in Montana. And if I hear another person tell me that today's young adults are materialistic and selfish, I'll just ask them to go to Catholic Extension's Web page and learn about those terrific kids from the suburbs who raced down to the bayous when their neighbors were in need. They are all vibrant testaments to the good work the Catholic Church is doing in our own land and among our own people.

Come and see: catholicextension.org

47

Catholic Relief Services

*Created in the image of God, all human life is sacred
and possesses a dignity that comes directly from our
creation and not from any action of our own.*
—From "Guiding Principles," Catholic Relief Services Website

Before you finish reading this paragraph, Catholic Relief
Services (CRS) will have rushed food, clothing, and medicine to tens of thousands of people struck by hurricane,
flood, or earthquake somewhere in the world. It will have
established community health programs in faraway lands
where there were no clinics, hospitals, or medicine, so that
people will have the tools they need to manage their own
health needs. In a world where a billion people don't have
access to a safe water supply, CRS will have helped people
in forty countries to take steps in meeting their basic
needs for water, health, and hygiene. In just three more
seconds CRS will have done much to improve the lives of
millions of people in more than one hundred countries
around the world.

Catholic Relief Services is the official international humanitarian agency of the Catholic community in the United States. Last year it touched the lives of 130 million people.

"Catholic Relief Services," writes Nicholas Kristof in the *New York Times*, "is one of the most vigorous aid organizations in the third world, and is an example of humanitarianism at its noblest."

Ninety-five percent of CRS's operating budget goes to programs. The American Institute of Philanthropy gives CRS an A rating. The *Chronicle of Philanthropy Annual* ranks it seventy-three in a list of four hundred. And the *NonProfit Times* ranks it number twenty-eight in the nation's top one hundred.

The U.S. Catholic bishops established CRS in 1943 to help refugees in war-torn Europe. Its first act was to find shelter in Mexico for 709 Polish refugees. Fifty years later, when war in Bosnia-Herzegovina killed two hundred thousand people and left more than two million refugees, CRS was there immediately with emergency assistance. It has evolved to provide long-term relief and development opportunities for people throughout the world.

CRS helps Catholics in the United States by giving them opportunities to express solidarity with their brothers and sisters everywhere, regardless of creed, race, or nationality. "CRS doesn't help the needy around the world so [that] we don't have to," observes Maryknoll Fr. Joseph Veneroso. "Rather, it gives us all occasions to help the poor through them. No organization in the church shows the worldwide face of the human family better than CRS. It invites all to the table. Literally."

Through Operation Rice Bowl, for instance, 12 million Catholic children and adults participate in a CRS program of prayer, fasting, and learning during Lent. CRS supplies parishes with meditations, recipes for simple meals, and stories that teach about life in the developing world. Families put monies into an empty rice bowl, a symbol of hunger that becomes a reality of love.

Cardinal James Hickey (1920–2004) of Washington, D.C., observed, "We don't help the poor because they are Catholic, we do because we are!"

The chosen part of Catholic Relief Services is a spiritual understanding of the Mystical Body of Christ. The U.S. bishops in *Called to Global Solidarity: International Challenges for U.S. Parishes* put it poignantly: "Through the eyes of faith, the starving child, the believer in jail, and the woman without clean water or health care are not issues but Jesus in disguise."

Jesus breathes in the AIDS patient kept alive by medicines from Catholic Relief Services. More than 80 million people in the world are infected with HIV and AIDS, and 25 million children have been orphaned. CRS is there for them. It operates 280 programs in 62 countries on three continents, working in partnership with other faith-based and nongovernmental organizations to give people affected by the epidemic a chance at life.

Jesus wears a burkha and walks in pink Crocs with other girls in a remote region of Afghanistan to a classroom started by Catholic Relief Services. There, under an open tent in the shade, she learns to read and write from local volunteers that CRS has trained to be teachers. She also takes part in CRS school feeding programs. CRS has supported these programs since 1958, not only to meet nutritional needs, but also to draw children, especially girls, to school.

Jesus in Pakistan, one of millions made homeless by a devastating flood, sleeps well for the first time in months under a makeshift roof on a bed mat given by Catholic Relief Services. In the morning he and his family will drink clean water and cook breakfast with kitchen supplies provided by CRS workers.

Jesus speaks through the voice of Fr. Joseph Mawa, pastor of St. Patrick's Church in Nimule, southern Sudan. "Peace is more than a ceasefire," he says. "It is freedom from fear, freedom from anxiety." Fr. Mawa holds peace-building meetings for children and their parents who have come from different tribes so they can learn to resolve their issues together and see that their spiritual bloodstreams trace back to a single pool of blood at the foot of a cross. Catholic Relief Services fosters peace building before conflict happens and is there to help healing after it does.

Jesus wears a bright orange sari in Baipariguda, India, where groups of self-employed women, usually the least-powerful people in a community, receive training and loans to grow their businesses, provide for their families, and give back to the community. Innovative CRS microfinance programs reach more than one million clients, 69.9 percent women, in thirty-six countries in five continents.

The huge outflow of love from those who wear the face of Christ in the United States has turned into food, water, sanitation, shelter, and medical care for nearly nine hundred thousand Haitians shaken by the 2010 earthquake. In Haiti CRS is also building thousands of transitional shelters—tough wooden homes built on a strong foundation—for families who can't yet rebuild the homes they lost. "We have worked in Haiti for more than fifty years," says CRS president Ken Hackett, "and we intend to remain alongside Haitians for many more years to come."

The work of CRS is nothing more and nothing less than a manifestation of Catholic ideas. It is action speaking louder than words. Elaine Menardi of Casper, Wyoming, who traveled to Ecuador with Catholic Relief Services in 2007 as part of its Called to Witness program, adapted and wrote a prayer that appears on the CRS website. It is one that each of us can pray on the spot where we're standing and be everywhere with the One who wears disguises but is one with the Father and with us all.

The Lord's Prayer (Little by Little, We Change the World, by Elaine Menardi)

In the eyes of the world, the strongest will survive.
In the eyes of God, the weakest will survive.

God always stands on the side of the meek and humble, and it is among the weak, that we find God. And so it is for all of us that we pray

Our Father . . .

Who is found among the lowly in the world—the poor, the vulnerable, those who struggle to love, the victims of circumstance and choice, the hidden ones among us.

who art in heaven . . .

A haven and refuge from pain, where the meek shall inherit the earth and the first shall be last, and the last shall be first.

hallowed be thy name . . .

Release us from our sinfulness that blinds us to the pain of our neighbor, that when we praise you, our hearts are filled with compassion and mercy.

thy Kingdom come . . .

Teach us to do justice, to love kindness, and to walk humbly with you that we might create a world where we reach beyond our own wants and desires.

thy will be done . . .

Open our eyes to let you in so that your perfect love may shine through us in all that we do.

on earth as it is in heaven . . .

May the work of our hands be the work of your hands that radiates your love for all, especially the poor.

give . . .

Us peace that surpasses all understanding that we may always hold up your command: Without cost, you have received; without cost, you are to give.

us . . .

The weak, the powerful; the rich, the poor; the neighbor, the foreigner; the sheltered, the homeless; the hungry, the well-fed . . . all these holy children of God that are one Body of Christ.

this day . . .

Not tomorrow, to make excuses and justify our wants when so many in the world survive on a handful of blessings.

our daily bread . . .

May each person in the world have enough to sustain a healthy life—food, clean water, clean air, shelter, health care, education and love.

and forgive us our trespasses . . .

Cure our blindness, forgive us for being preoccupied with ourselves, and teach us to see you in the faces of others.

as we forgive those . . .

Teach us to be generous with our forgiveness that we may not hold back any hurt or anger towards another, but be genuine in reconciling broken relationships.

who trespass against us . . .

Fill us with your grace that dissolves bitterness, resentment and pain; and do not let us waste days on anger or hatred.

and lead us not into temptation . . .

Be patient with our humanity, for we will fail many times; instead, give us more days to learn to feed the hungry, clothe the naked, and visit the prisoner; trying to mend oppressive systems that render vulnerable the lowly.

but deliver us from evil . . .
From the sin that keeps us comfortable and allows us to continue with our lives blind to the pain and suffering of our brothers and sisters around the world.

for the kingdom . . .
This world that you gave for everyone, not just the rich and powerful, but the meek and humble, and especially the poor.

the power . . .
May we be right users of power, claiming an option for the poor and those who have no voice, using our power to shift the balance of wealth toward equity for all.

and the glory . . .
Let them see not me, but only You shining through me.

are yours . . .
You are the only one worthy of glory, and we give it all to you.

now and forever . . .
Until the end of days, you are our God.

Amen . . .
We believe it so—that we will see the coming of the glory of the Lord.

Come and see: www.crs.org

48

Catholic Books and Bookstores

Beware the man of one book.
—THOMAS AQUINAS

I love the smell of cinnamon in the morning. I love the smell of the ocean in the afternoon. I love the smell of apple-scented candlelight at night. And, most of all, I love the smell of old books!

Even though they smell like dust.

I've been writing, editing, and publishing Catholic books for the past forty years, so I probably smell like a 1966 Dutch Catechism. A 1966 Dutch Catechism smells like an old wooden shoe.

When I was a kid, I borrowed books from two different libraries but loved riding my Schwinn to a used bookstore on North Broadway with a storefront window that always displayed old and mysterious books. I'd chain my bike to a lamppost, enter the quiet store, and trip out into new worlds. I solved mysteries with the Hardy Boys, sailed through storms with Jack London, and swung from tree to tree with Tarzan and Jane. I also went on holy adventures with saints in books such as *Damien the Leper, Joan of Arc,* and *Saint Francis of the Seven Seas.* You could buy books like that for a dime. The Music Box, my neighborhood movie show, cost fifteen cents. Books that play in your mind longer than a movie have always been a bargain!

When I was fourteen, I entered Quigley Preparatory Seminary because I wanted to be a priest. In the back of the old bookstore, under "Occult," I found a big fat book on Catholic apologetics that promised to help me confound anyone who didn't believe what I did. My Uncle Barney was an atheist, so I tested out my new knowledge on him. I remember one argument during which Uncle Barney said that someday scientists would be able to create human beings in a laboratory. I told him that was Frankenstein talk, and anyway only God can make a tree! I was obnoxious, and have never liked apologetics since. Uncle Barney was not a bad guy, and if he were alive today, he'd probably resist the temptation to say, "See, I told you so," about those lab babies.

I got a comeuppance when I was fifteen and came across a book by an ex-priest who had a beef with the church. Since I could think of no better vocation for me than the priesthood—other than playing center field for the Cubs—I bought the thirty-five-cent book out of curiosity. It shook me up like a Don Drysdale fastball to the head. I learned about the Inquisition and the Crusades and popes who made their babies popes! and all kinds of crimes and misdemeanors. My Catholic guilt erupted like a zit the size of Vesuvius. I knew I'd go to hell just for reading it. So I went to confession to Fr. Ciezadlo, the kindest priest I knew.

He not only absolved me but didn't make a federal case out of it. "If your faith is built on a foundation of truth," he seemed to say, "nothing can hurt it. Don't be afraid."

The book didn't hurt my faith; it made me more interested in seeking truth. And the truth was, I learned later that the guy who wrote the book was on target about a lot of things. Since that time I've read and given away thousands of Catholic and other religious books with many points of view, and each one has one way or another enriched my faith. The only thing I'd rather be than Catholic is center fielder for the Cubs.

When I was sixteen, the bookstore on Broadway closed, but a brand-new Catholic bookstore opened in downtown Chicago, the Thomas More Bookstore. It was the world's greatest candy store of Catholic books. I was working weekends and summers as an Andy Frain usher at Cubs, Bears, and Blackhawk games, so I had plenty of money to buy books and see movies at the Music Box. I loved the rack of Image Books, a line of classics published by Doubleday editor John Delaney. They had *Mr. Blue, The Diary of a Country Priest,* and *Practicing the Presence of God,* books by Fulton Sheen, G. K. Chesterton, and Thomas Merton, classics from Augustine, John of the Cross, and Theresa of Ávila. They also had a whole table of Catholic novels with covers that created an instant love affair with anyone passing by. I experienced *The Power and the Glory* with Graham Greene, tasted *Wise Blood* with Flannery O'Connor, and walked on *The Edge of Sadness* with Edwin O'Connor. The Thomas More Bookstore, an Aladdin's castle of Catholic literature, closed years ago, but you can still smell the bouquet of books when you walk past the building on Wabash Avenue.

Today Catholics can keep their Schwinns in the basement and get any book they wish in a flash from amazon.com or barnesandnoble.com, or they can visit a spacious Barnes and Noble or Borders superstore at the nearest mall. Or they can visit a friendly Catholic book–and-gift shop that smells like bells and offers a wide selection of books, cards, art, and music. A model for the new Catholic stores is the gift shop at the Cathedral of Our Lady of the Angels in Los Angeles. The cathedral, third largest in the world, offers Mass in forty-two different languages and is the mother church to 4 million Catholics. Its shop offers parishioners and downtown neighbors a wide variety of books and gifts, ranging from five-dollar rosaries strung with ruby-colored glass beads to porcelain sculptures of Jesus, Mary, and the saints.

Isabel Loriente, manager of the shop, points out what the good folks at the Thomas More Bookstore knew when the march of time forced them to close their doors: "In today's changing world, books barely make a profit. Catholics also desire sacramental objects that remind them of the sacred in life, and these gifts support the books. The profits then go to the church's mission. Everyone benefits." Isabel, like many managers or owners of Catholic stores, was drawn to her vocation through a back door. As a little girl from a nonreligious family, she went to church alone and loved to spend time in the tiny shop tucked away in the vestibule. "It was both a guilty pleasure and a comfort," she remembers. "I'd hold a figurine of the Blessed Mother and look at her peaceful gaze and know that somehow, someway I was safe. I'd study the saints on holy cards and see valor and generosity. I'd read from spiritual books and begin to understand that God wants only good for me and everyone, no matter what things look like. Everything I saw or touched in that little shop reminded me that there's so much more to this world than meets the eye. Now I love to share with customers the *Aha!* of a new book I read or just listen to their questions and concerns and be as helpful and open as I can."

Some fifteen hundred Catholic book-and-gift shops around the country offer this kind of service. Some of the larger ones are Newman Bookstore in D.C., Sikora's Bookstore in Passaic, New Jersey, the Shrine of Queen of the Universe in Orlando, Watra Religious Books and Gifts in Chicago, St. Patrick's Guild in Minneapolis, Viva in San Antonio, the Paulist Press Book Center in Costa Mesa, and Kaufer's in Seattle. The Daughters of St. Paul have fifteen Pauline Book and Media Centers. To find a Catholic bookstore near you, go online to the Catholic Marketing Network (*catholicmarketing.com*) or the Catholic Retailer's Association (*catholicretailers.com*) and follow the bouncing ball.

There are also two hundred publishers of Catholic books in the country. You can learn about them by going to the Association of Catholic Book Publishers at *www.cbpa.com*. Some of the book publishers Catholics have traditionally relied on for excellence are those associated with religious orders: Loyola Press (Jesuits); Orbis

Books (Maryknoll); Paulist Press (Paulists); Liturgical Press (St. John's Abbey); Ave Maria Press (Holy Cross); St. Anthony Messenger Press (Franciscans); Ligouri Publications (Redemptorists); ACTA Publications (Assisting Christians to Act); Liturgy Training Publications (Archdiocese of Chicago); and USCCB Publishing (U.S. Bishops). All of these publishers, and the 190 others, have excellent books you won't find reviewed in your local newspaper or favorite magazine, but they will inform, inspire, and enlighten you, and remind you why it's worthwhile to stay Catholic.

You can also pay attention to your Sunday church bulletin, and when the parish offers a speaker on a weekday evening, surprise yourself and attend. Some of the best Catholic authors in the country give great talks on weekday evenings in parishes throughout the country. Chances are you've read a book by James Patterson or Anne Tyler or Chelsea Handler, but has anyone told you about James Martin or Joyce Rupp or Richard Rohr? They are topselling Catholic authors who often speak at parishes and who would delight and enlighten you. If you suspect there is more to Catholicism than you've read or heard about, a little research will lead you to a book or study group or conference that can lead you beyond statements about the truth to the Truth that will set you free. "When the student is ready," an old saying goes, "the teacher will come." It may not happen all at once, it may include detours, and it may include insight from non-Catholic texts that open the doors to understanding, but it is guaranteed. God reveals himself to those who do not ask for him, and is found by those who do not even seek him. Jesus promises that those who seek shall find even faster (Matthew 7:8).

Somebody once asked theologian Karl Rahner, "Will the Catholic book have a future?" Rahner said, "It will be transformed, but it will endure. It will achieve this even if it takes the form of an unending variation upon the single basic theme: 'My God, my God, why have you forsaken me?' Even then it will endure and will lead us to that point in our human existence at which this existence is thrown headlong into the redeeming mystery."

You may find the answer or a beautiful clue in an old book that smells like dust or a new one that smells like motor oil. Maybe the Way will appear on a screen with pixels you hold in your hand or, the day after tomorrow, implanted on the inside of your eyelids. But always heed the words of Aquinas, and do not become "a man of one book." Have fun, be adventurous, and as Fr. Ciezadlo advised, "Don't be afraid!"

Come and see: catholicmarketing.com and catholicretailers.com and cbpa.com

49

The Los Angeles Religious Education Congress

If you build it, he will come.
—*FIELD OF DREAMS*

We all know the startling statistics. The average age of a priest is 101, and all three of them are having nervous breakdowns doing baptisms, weddings, and funerals in New York, Chicago, and Los Angeles. The average Catholic now gives no percentage of his income to the church and is instead asking for a refund. The average Catholic teenager goes to church fewer times than the average old person goes to a Justin Bieber concert.

Is it over?

"Over? Did you say 'over?'" asked John Belushi in *Animal House.* "Nothing is over until we decide it is! Was it over when the Germans bombed Pearl Harbor? No!"

And Sr. Edith Prendergast agrees. She and her colleagues at the Office for Religious Education at the Archdiocese of Los Angeles make things happen.

Director of the office since 1987, Sr. Edith leads the annual LA Religious Education Congress that blossoms in Anaheim every spring. It is a model for church, and makes you glad to be Catholic. For four days, twenty-five thousand Catholic adults and sixteen thousand teenagers—singing and sharing their faith—shake the rafters of the Anaheim Convention Center, a block away from Disneyland. People flock to Congress not only from California and states as far away as New York, but from Canada, Mexico, Latin America, the Philippines, Australia, Vietnam, England, Ireland, and Africa. It is a world's fair of Catholicism. "It takes a year for our staff to plan and involves the generosity of five hundred volunteers," says Sr. Edith, "but those four days always go smoothly. Congress is a microcosm of what the church can be when it commits itself to the vision that grace really abounds."

The chosen part of the LA Congress—its spiritual foundation—is fearless celebration of the diverse gifts in the church (1 Corinthians 12:3–5). In three days it offers close to three hundred workshops presented by more than two hundred top Catholic speakers. Topics range from theology to Scripture to spirituality—in English, Spanish, and Vietnamese. You can attend any and as many as you wish. The Congress provides fourteen diverse Eucharistic liturgies treasured by Catholics, including African American, Native American, Byzantine, Celtic, Indonesian, Nigerian, Spanish, Vietnamese, Contemplative, Gregorian, and Young Adult, as well as evening prayer and other services. After all, the archdiocese celebrates liturgy every Sunday in no fewer than forty different languages, and Congress reflects the church. In 2010 more than twenty thousand people attended the final liturgies, which featured the talents of 275 musicians and a choir of two hundred singers from six dioceses, including thirty students from six colleges and universities. If singing is praying twice, as Augustine said, then going to Mass at Congress is truly the prayer of angels.

And there is more.

Each year the huge hall showcases the gifts and ministries of two hundred Catholic exhibitors—ranging from religious orders to educational institutions, book publishers to gift companies and individual artists. The hall is a spiritual marketplace so valued by the forty thousand attendees that the aisles overflow with shoppers and vocation seekers and friends looking for friends they see but once a year at Congress. I've been going since 1980 and can tell you that no other event in the course of a year inspires me more or gives me more energy to go back and do my work than the LA Congress. The people there are the grace that abounds, and they fill my heart with joy.

"I look forward to coming to Congress because it's like a vitamin B shot of spirituality for me," says Kay Easley, a confirmation minister at St. Elizabeth Ann Seton Church in Fort Collins, Colorado. "I just appreciate so many wonderful speakers with so many deep, good thoughts that I can think about when I get home and share in my ministries in our church."

Pat Marinier, an RCIA leader and lector from Yacolt, Washington, says, "The first year I went to see what I could learn—head stuff. The second year I went to nourish my spirit. Now I just soak up the joy of being Catholic. I rub elbows with those who know what is in my bones and understand the place I come from. My spirituality is no longer a head-heart thing. It is just *being*, no duality anymore. As Richard Rohr says, 'Everything belongs!'"

Congress opens on a Thursday with a daylong event for sixteen thousand high school youth. Students come not only from the archdiocese but throughout California and the western states and literally have fun celebrating their faith. They help prepare the liturgy, perform the music, and share in the homily with the cardinal. Some students learn leadership skills so they can go back to their parishes and be the "salt of the earth" (Matthew 5:13). But most of all, everyone hears the ideas that matter most. Nadia Torres, a student from Sacred Heart High School in Lincoln Heights, told the *Los Angeles Tidings*, "Fr. Tony's talk made me realize that God is there for us. My Father is someone I can go to if anything goes wrong."

"God is everywhere and he will help you through everything," said Safiya Al-Sarraf, a Muslim from Sierra Madre's Alverno High School. "The whole experience is not a message only for Catholics," said her Muslim friend and classmate Lana El-Farra. "It is a universal message and I can also get something out of it." Kimberly Ruano, a Sacred Heart ninth grader, said it all: "I feel like this is one big family."

The Archdiocese of Los Angeles is committed to the family of God. It makes it possible for young people such as Kimberly to experience the joy of being Catholic with friends at a nominal contribution of $20. An all-day visit to Disneyland costs a minimum of $76. Adults pay only $60 for three days of *everything* at the Congress. The money that the Archdiocese puts into this annual event is an expression of love.

"Love unfolding is the way of Jesus," says Sr. Edith. "He called his disciples to 'come and see' and calls us into deeper friendship and interconnection with him and with all of life. That's what Congress is about—this bond of oneness, this fastening of the spirit to a loving God!"

Come and see: www.recongress.org and *Grace Abounds* by Edith Prendergast

50

Vatican III

Consult not your fears but your hopes and your dreams.
Think not about your frustrations, but about your unfulfilled
potential. Concern yourself not with what you tried and
failed in, but with what it is still possible for you to do.
—POPE JOHN XXIII, VATICAN II (1962)

"Vatican II was a force that seized the mind of the Roman
Catholic Church and carried it across centuries from the
13th to the 20th," wrote Lance Morrow in *Time* magazine.
When Pope John opened the windows of the church, he
not only let new ideas in; he also let beautiful birds out
that had been trapped inside! Those birds were spiritual
ideas that were caged for centuries in favor of parrots that
repeated the same words over and over again. The birds
began singing new songs that were variations on age-old
melodies. Catholics listened and heard, and they, too,
"sang a new song" (Psalm 144:9). It was a time of harmony.

But times change. Today the church is in one of those
periods that come and go when birds of a feather do not

flock together. The church, like the world, is polarized. Is it time for a Vatican III?

Sure, why not? It's also time for something completely different. The 2,860 bishops who met in Rome for three years drafted sixteen seminal documents on the church, liturgy, ministry, Scripture, revelation, religious education, religious freedom, ecumenism, social justice, and much more. They were historic. But do we need any more statements *about* Catholicism?

Please let me suggest something that can lift the church from the twentieth century to the twenty-first century, not in three years but in three days. Something that can take place not just in the Vatican but in every Catholic church in the world—all at the same time!

A forgiveness ceremony.

Here is how it will work.

The pope begins to make the crooked paths straight (Luke 3:5) three months in advance by releasing a short encyclical on forgiveness (one thousand words), emphasizing the core Catholic truth that nothing—*nothing*, not even sin—can separate us from the love of God (Romans 8:38–39). He reminds us of the words of Pope John Paul II: "The love of Christ is more powerful than sin and death. St. Paul explains that Christ came to forgive sin and that his love is greater than any sin, stronger than all my personal sins or those of anyone else. This is the faith of the church. This is the Good News of God's love that the Church proclaims throughout history and that I proclaim to you today: God loves you with an everlasting love. He loves you in Christ Jesus, his Son!"

The new encyclical begs forgiveness on behalf of the church for all those it has hurt, living and dead, and vows to reform itself. It forgives and asks forgiveness from all the good Catholics, living and dead, who did not have the means to get annulments and so divorced and remarried, and encourages them to receive communion again.

For three months priests preach forgiveness, no strings attached, from the pulpits. They repeat the Catholic truth: no matter what we do or how bad we think we are, nothing can separate us from the love of God. Just as no one or nothing can separate a wave from the ocean or a sunbeam from the sun, nothing and no one can separate us from the God in whom "we live and move and have our being" (Acts 17:28). We are not human beings struggling to become spiritual; we are spiritual beings who have forgotten what and where we really are.

During these three months the church reaches into the attic of Catholic consciousness to release the white dove that says, "Your sins have become white as snow!" (Isaiah 1:18). The church focuses on the chosen part of salvation and recalls Jesus' assurance: "I am in my Father, and you in me, and I in you. . . . Do not let your hearts be troubled, and do not be afraid!" (John 14:20, 27, NIV). It reminds us that when Jesus saved the adulteress about to be stoned, he didn't say, "Sin no more and I will not condemn you." He said, "I do not condemn you. *Now* go and sin no more!" We *first* experience God's love, and *then* our life changes forever. Guilt makes sin, and sin makes guilt, and guilt makes more sin to escape more guilt. Forgiveness makes love, and love makes us forgive others.

Love begins, and grows, with forgiveness, unearned and freely given.

In this encyclical the pope announces a three-day forgiveness ceremony on the first weekend of Lent. On the Friday and Saturday of that weekend, three times each day, a parish priest leads the assembly to take hold of our sins and empty our hands of them to God, who is unconditional Love being constantly loving. As we examine our conscience, we become aware that we still hold others, living and dead, in bondage to our resentments. The priest guides us to see these individuals, one by one, in our mind's eye, and we pray within:

> Father, forgive me my trespasses as I forgive those who have trespassed against me. Give me the grace to forgive, right now, all those I still blame. If those who hurt me only knew who both of us really are, they would not have done what they did. (Name), I forgive you and set you free. (Name), I forgive you and set us both free!

Then the priest witnesses to God's overwhelming love by offering a general absolution to everyone in the church. The priest does this with the blessing and encouragement of the pope. Forgiveness becomes an almighty force that opens hearts, cleanses minds, and inspires our whole being. Just like the adulterer, the people are free to go and sin no more! Everybody starts from scratch. This is the only way the church—or anyone—can be born again.

On the third day, at Sunday Eucharist, the forgiveness ceremony continues with readings and prayers that further reorient the assembly to lives of compassion and forgiveness. They learn again that they cannot escape Love:

> Wither shall I go from thy spirit? Or wither shall I flee from thy presence? If I ascend up into heaven, thou art there: if I make my bed in hell, behold thou art there. If I take the wings of the morning, and dwell in the uttermost parts of the sea, even there shall thy hand lead me and thy right hand shall hold me! (Psalm 139:7–10, NKJ)

The assembly understands that it is realization of *love*, not fear, that "leads us not into temptation." They express gratitude.

At the Lord's Prayer, everyone looks at his or her neighbor and says, "Forgive me." Forgiveness received, they say in kind, "I forgive you."

At the end of the Mass the priest says, "Go and give what God has given you!"

Forgiveness—the recognition that what the church has always taught, that we are all children of God, brothers and sisters of Christ, and heirs of heaven, and nothing can change that—becomes the theme of the church. It forgives and asks forgiveness of those it has excommunicated: the theologians who have dissented; the bishops who said Latin Masses when told not to; the hospital sister in Phoenix who saved a mother's life but was accused of abortion; every woman, living or dead, who has made the gut-wrenching, life-shattering decision to have an abortion. All free. Free to love and be loved again. By practicing what it preaches, the church not only draws more people to a loving God but also is able to reach out to other religions without wanting anything in return.

By remembering what it has forgotten, by emphasizing what it has neglected, the church becomes like Jesus.

Little miracles begin to happen. The liberal Call to Action group invites members of the conservative Opus Dei to their annual conference and asks some of their leaders to speak and engage in dialogue with the attendees. They eat together. Mother Angelica's Eternal Word Network invites Catholics it previously criticized to be guests and talk with them about Jesus. Forgiveness becomes paramount in Catholic consciousness. Ideas are energy, and energy transforms itself into other forms of energy: words, behavior, healings. People treat one another with respect. Peace extinguishes anger; love overcomes fear. The consciousness of forgiveness becomes a collective consciousness, and someday, who knows, the Cosmic consciousness that has always been here. And someday, who knows, the words of Teilhard de Chardin, will come to life!

> Someday, after mastering the winds, the waves, the tides and gravity, we shall harness for God the energies of love, and then, for a second time in the history of the world, man will have discovered fire!

Come and see: www.whystaycatholic.com

Thank You's

Thank you, Loyola Press—especially you, Joe Durepos, for never taking no for a final answer; Tom McGrath for your friendship; Steve Connor for your enthusiasm; and Vinita Hampton Wright for not only knowing what it means to be a good editor but for being one of the great ones. Great big thanks to all the other artists and pros at Loyola who worked so lovingly to make this a beautiful, reader-friendly book and then make it public with gusto. It has been a wonderful publishing experience. Thanks, too, to all my friends—too many to fit on a page—whom I asked to lend a hand. You know who you are—please know that I am grateful from the bottom of my heart.

About the Author

MICHAEL LEACH is publisher emeritus and editor-at-large of Orbis Books. A leader in Catholic publishing for thirty years, he has edited and published more than two thousand books. His authors include Nobel Prize winners, National Book Award winners, and hundreds of Catholic Book Award winners. He has served as president of the Catholic Book Publishers Association and the ecumenical Religion Publishers Group. Before joining Orbis as publisher in 1997 he was president of the Crossroad Publishing Company in New York City. In 2007 the Catholic Book Publishers Association honored him with a Lifetime Achievement Award. Dubbed "the dean of Catholic book publishing" by *U.S. Catholic* magazine, he has authored or edited several books of his own, including the bestseller *I Like Being Catholic* and *A Maryknoll Book of Prayer, The People's Catechism,* and *I Like Being Married.* A popular speaker at conferences nationwide, Michael lives in Connecticut with Vickie, his wife of forty-two years.